D0216721

THE DEVELOPMENT OF SOCIAL SENSITIVITY

The development of social sensitivity

A STUDY OF SOCIAL ASPECTS OF ROLE-TAKING IN YOUNG CHILDREN

Paul Light

LECTURER IN PSYCHOLOGY, UNIVERSITY OF SOUTHAMPTON

Cambridge University Press

CAMBRIDGE

LONDON · NEW YORK · MELBOURNE

Published by the Syndics of the Cambridge University Press
The Pitt Building, Trumpington Street, Cambridge CB2 1RP
Bentley House, 200 Euston Road, London NW1 2DB
32 East 57th Street, New York, NY 10022, USA
296 Beaconsfield Parade, Middle Park, Melbourne 3206, Australia

First published 1979

Printed in Great Britain at the
University Press, Cambridge

ISBN 0 521 223725

TO VIVIENNE

CONTENTS

LIST OF TABLES

LIST OF FIGURES

PREFACE

The central concern of this book is with individual differences in the extent to which preschool children engage in social role-taking. In other words, our concern is with how far the child takes account of other people's perceptions, expectations or emotions in his dealings with them. Role-taking is considered in relation to other aspects of the child's thinking, and also in relation to the child's own social behaviour. There is a dearth of research on the relationship between the child's understanding of other people and his actual social behaviour, so much so in fact that this has been referred to as 'one of the largest unexplored areas in developmental psychology today' (Shantz, 1975). As well as going some way toward filling this gap, the research reported in this book provides evidence bearing on the important question of the origin of individual differences in role-taking. Such differences are shown to be systematically related to rather subtle aspects of mother–child interaction. The findings of the present study may provide a firmer starting point than has been available in the past for integrative research on the socialisation of thought in early childhood.

The research upon which this book is based was conducted as part of a larger research programme directed by Martin Richards at the Unit for Research into Medical Applications of Psychology in Cambridge. The programme was supported at various stages by the Nuffield Foundation, The Mental Health Research Fund, and the Social Science Research Council. Judy Dunn, Frances Barnes and Barbara Antonis have all been involved in the research and I am grateful to them, as well as to Martin Richards, for their willingness to let me draw upon their work and for the help and encouragement they have given. My thanks are due also to the parents and children involved in the study, who gave so freely of their time, and finally to my wife for her help in the preparation of the manuscript.

1

'No Man is an island, entire of itself'†

The research framework

Psychological research on children, particularly preschool and early school-age children, has in recent years been largely dominated by the 'cognitive-developmental' approach. This approach, which directly reflects the influence of Jean Piaget, is concerned primarily with cognitive or logical competence, and with the supposedly invariant sequences of stages in the development of such competence. Lawrence Kohlberg (1969) provides a lucid discussion of this paradigm. The research upon which this book is based has been influenced by the cognitive-developmental approach, but differs in its emphases from most of the work in the field. Firstly, the present research concentrates upon the child's thinking about his social environment, rather than his understanding of the physical, nonsocial environment. Secondly, the focus will be on individual differences in observed behaviour, and on the factors which might be responsible for such differences. In line with its epistemological aims, cognitive-developmental theory has inclined towards abstract and general models of cognitive change, giving little insight into the effective conditions for development at the individual level. Consequently, the vast majority of studies concern groups of children at several age levels, with the emphasis on between-group comparisons. The research reported in this volume concerns a single sample of children. Comparisons are made within the group on a wide variety of indices, relating to the children themselves and to their families. This detailed, individualised approach permits much greater insight both into individual differences and idiosyncrasies, and into the range of interpersonal contexts within which the children are functioning.

† John Donne, *Devotions*

Social and cognitive development

Social role-taking was chosen as the focus of this research because of its potential as a bridging concept, linking the traditional domains of social and cognitive development. Before social role-taking can be adequately defined and its significance understood, a rather detailed consideration of the theoretical background to this question of the relation of social and cognitive development will be necessary.

Piaget is often singled out as being responsible for the separation of these two aspects of development, but actually he has himself argued that social and intellectual developments are intimately related (e.g. Piaget and Inhelder, 1969). Indeed they are seen as running in parallel, such parallelism being one of the more generally held notions amongst cognitive-developmental theorists (see Kohlberg, 1969). To understand why it has not led to more integration of research on social and cognitive development requires a more critical examination of Piaget's writings on the subject.

Besides Piaget's, the most influential viewpoint on this question is probably that of George Herbert Mead (1863–1931). Mead regarded rationality as a peculiarly social construct, its emergence in the individual being entirely dependent upon prior social experience (Mead, 1934). A comparison of Mead's position with Piaget's shows up many fundamental similarities of view, but also important differences of emphasis. A close consideration of these two theoretical positions will provide a broad context within which to consider the research to be reported in subsequent chapters.

Piaget's concept of egocentrism

Piaget (e.g. 1926) describes the initial state of the child's thinking as 'autistic', being totally individualistic and asocial. The final state of thinking he labels 'directed', directed thought being social in that it involves accommodating to others' points of view. The transitional condition between these two extremes Piaget terms 'egocentric' thought. The essence of egocentrism is the child's embeddedness in his own point of view; only his own point of view, *his* schemas, *his* perceptions etc. really figure in his activities, and he is unaware that others see things differently. The child is thus unaware of having a point of view, as opposed to having a direct grasp of reality. Since, according to Piaget, his knowledge about the world derives from his own actions, it is not surprising that the child begins by thinking of things in terms of his own subjective activity.

Egocentrism refers, then, to the child's centering on his own actions and his own point of view in his dealings with the world. It represents Piaget's attempt to resolve the relationships of social and individual factors in the early and middle childhood periods.

The concept of egocentrism had so central a place in Piaget's early writings (e.g. 1926, 1928) that Vygotsky, in a work originally published in 1934, summarised them thus: 'According to Piaget, the bond uniting all the specific characteristics of child logic is the egocentrism of the child's thinking. To this core trait he relates all the other traits he found' (1962, p. 11). In later work on intellectual development Piaget continued to give a central place to egocentrism (e.g. Piaget, 1950; Inhelder and Piaget, 1958). Egocentrism was invoked as an explanation of a wide variety of children's behaviours during the preschool and early school-age period. Since he has never written a systematic account of the concept of egocentrism, we shall need to briefly examine the uses to which he puts it in a variety of contexts.

Since the egocentric child continually assimilates reality to his own perspective, he confuses subjective justification with verification, and similarly confuses motives with causes. Piaget's term 'precausality' includes all forms of causality based upon a confusion between psychological activity and physical mechanism. Related to this are three 'reality notions'. Realism describes a tendency to substantiate psychological events or products (names, dreams, thoughts etc.) – to see them as *things*. Animism describes the converse tendency to endow physical things with life, supposing consciousness or will. Artificialism describes the belief that all objects in the world were made by man or for man's purposes.

The idea of nominal realism is nicely exemplified by Vygotsky's anecdote about a man who could understand that the astronomers could work out the sizes and paths of all the planets, but was very puzzled by how they found out their names! Piaget and Inhelder (1969) give an example of artificialism: a six year old asked 'Why are there two Mount Salèves?' (The Great Salève and the Little Salève.) Piaget asked the child's contemporaries what they thought, and almost all replied: 'one for big trips and one for little trips'.

Moral notions of equity are not possible for the egocentric child as they require the other person's point of view to be taken into account, and depend on reciprocal relations between those involved. So the preschool child reifies the prohibitions of adults: the child's moral realism reflects a lack of distinction between a moral stricture and a state of nature. The lack of distinction between motives and causes leads to judgements of culpability in terms of consequence, irrespective of intention (Piaget, 1932).

Difficulty in exchanging information is another aspect of the child's egocentrism. The child finds it difficult or unnecessary to impart information to another since he cannot take the part of one who does not know what he knows. A great deal of the child's talk is 'talk for self', even when in the company of others. Piaget considers that this 'egocentric speech', if it has a communicative aim at all, is inadequate because there is no real attempt to take the role of the listener in order to adapt the message to his informational needs – and often no attempt to make sure that he is even listening.

Symbolic play marks the purest form of egocentrism for Piaget, since in symbolic play reality is freely assimilated to the child's own schemata.

In order to see how the concept of egocentrism relates social behaviour to individual cognitive development in this period, a quick sketch of Piaget's account of preoperational thinking will be necessary. The thinking of the preschool child is, for Piaget, organised in terms of 'preconcepts' which tend to be imagistic and concrete rather than schematic and abstract. As Flavell (1963) puts it, they refer neither to individuals who possess a stable identity over time and in different contexts nor to genuine classes or collectives of similar individuals. There is difficulty in recognising stable identity in different contexts and difficulty in seeing similar members of a given class as distinct and different individuals.

It is characteristic of the child's reasoning at this time to center on some salient element of an event and to proceed to draw from it, as conclusion, some other perceptually compelling happening ('transduction'). Elements are thus juxtaposed associatively rather than causally and in this way almost anything can be related to anything else ('syncretism').

Judgements made regarding, say, number are made either by reference to a single perceived aspect of a situation (e.g. the equality in length of two rows of buttons), or by reference to the child's own action (in making these rows the same length). Similarly, in the 'classic' situation of nonconservation of continuous quantity involving the pouring of liquid between differently shaped beakers, the child's judgement is determined by a single perceptual dimension of the situation – he may for instance, center on water level and judge simply by this criterion. This 'centering' of thought is also reflected in the use of descriptions which mention only one dimension of an array and which use absolute rather than relative terms to describe it.

Piaget uses the term 'preoperational' to characterise the child's thinking in this period, between the end of the sensorimotor period (about 2 years) and the beginning of the construction of concrete operations (about 7 years). The account of preoperational thinking given above shows that it depends for its properties on one unifying feature – that it is *centered*. This 'centering' takes two main forms: centering in reasoning on single, perceptually striking characteristics of objects or events, and centering on the self to the exclusion of others' points of view. Langer (1969) has suggested the term 'perspectivism' to describe these linked phenomena: the child's progressive capacity to differentiate cognitively amongst several aspects of an event and likewise to differentiate between his own and others' points of view. Although the latter is nearer to what we normally understand by 'egocentrism', it is important to recognise that Piaget subsumes both these aspects of 'centering' in his use of the term.

According to Piaget, the construction of transitive and reversible ('operational') thinking involves the conversion of this initial egocentrism into a series of relations and classes which are decentralised with respect to the self. The whole of early childhood is seen in terms of this process of decentralisation: he describes it as 'a long integrated process that may be characterised as a transition from subjective centering in all areas to a decentering that is at once cognitive, social and moral' (Piaget and Inhelder, 1969, p. 128).

In summary, then, Piaget is arguing that the same processes (or at least parallel processes) are involved in both impersonal and interpersonal cognition. In the social domain the young child has to develop from a 'one track' mentality to one in which he is able to move flexibly and reversibly from one perspective to another, so that effective social communication and cooperation become possible. The young child is also 'one track' in the strictly intellectual domain, but as he achieves concrete operations his thinking shows increasing flexibility and reversibility. The ability of the child to 'decenter' his attention permits the realisation that situations may have several covarying features, and also permits the realisation that an object would appear differently if viewed from another perspective.

The role of social experience

We have seen that for Piaget social reciprocity or reversibility corresponds to the intellectual reversibility which characterises operational thinking, and that egocentrism signifies the absense of both of these forms of reversibility. How, then, is egocentrism overcome during the preoperational period? In his early writings Piaget clearly took the view that the recognition of inter-individual reciprocity was achieved by the child directly through social experience, and that intellectual decentration followed from social decentration: 'In fact, it is precisely by a constant interchange of thought with others that we are able to decentralise ourselves in this way' (Piaget, 1950, p. 164).

He emphasised the peer group as a situation in which the child would be repeatedly confronted by alternative views. The resulting conflicts and arguments were seen by Piaget as forcing the child to re-examine his own percepts in the light of those of others. Flavell, in 1963, described as 'one of Piaget's firmest beliefs' that egocentrism is overcome only through repeated interpersonal interactions in which the child is actually forced again and again to take cognisance of the role of the other. It was this process that Piaget had in mind when he declared that 'logical thought is necessarily social' (1950, p. 165).

However, the attribution of a clear causal role to social experience is not evident in Piaget's more recent writings. In Piaget (1965) and Piaget and Inhelder (1969) the argument is made that operational thinking and directed social behaviour develop hand in hand, being two aspects of a single reality within which it is impossible to separate cause from effect. This equivocal position leaves open the possibility that social experience and behaviour affect individual cognitive development, but equally leaves open the opposite direction of effects. At times Piaget seems to go further, suggesting that developments in the interpersonal sphere simply reflect individual cognitive development: 'When he [the child] reaches the level of operations, he will by that very fact be capable of cooperation' (Piaget and Inhelder, 1969, p. 129).

This position seems the most consistent with Piaget's recent work, in which he has made scant reference either to the development of social behaviour or to the interdependence of intelligent behaviour and experience in a social context. Thus in practice he has tended to preserve the isolated-individual approach which has so frequently characterised the study of cognitive development. Although Piaget is clearly not categorically denying the significance of social experience in the development of thinking, his recent work contains few, if any, suggestions concerning the crucial factors in such experience or the nature of their effects upon the child's development.

An alternative standpoint on egocentrism

Piaget was heavily criticised for his 'individualist' position by Henri Wallon in the 1940s (Wallon, 1947, Voyat, 1973). The preceding paragraphs have essentially echoed Wallon's criticism, that although Piaget acknowledged the importance of the social milieu, he ignored its systematic study.

Wallon emphasised an alternative perspective on the phenomena which Piaget had described under the heading of egocentrism. Wallon's interest was in the child's growing awareness of his own ego; in the process of individualisation rather than socialisation. He was interested in the reflective self awareness which he saw as growing out of the fusion of self-as-subject with self-as-social-object; what he called the 'I am me' phenomenon. Piaget, centering on the individual, interprets the changes the child undergoes as a growing awareness of the other and of the group. Wallon saw the same changes as reflecting the child's movement from an initial kind of symbiosis towards an increasing awareness of self as distinct from other. The differentiation of self from other results in an awareness of one's own personality. Wallon's criticisms of Piaget are very close to those intended by Vygotsky when he said 'the true direction of the development of thinking is not from the individual to the socialised but from the social to the individual' (1962, p. 20).

Subsequently (1950, 1955) Piaget has himself acknowledged that the concept of egocentrism has profound implications for the child's self awareness or self knowledge. The child, he says: 'is egocentric through ignorance of his own subjectivity' (1950, p. 160). Moreover, reflecting upon his disagreements with Wallon, Piaget has suggested (Piaget and Inhelder, 1969) that the opposing sides were in fact saying almost the same thing. The difference is perhaps one of emphasis, but the difference in emphasis is important.

Wallon's writings made little impact in the English speaking world, but closely related ideas about the construction of individual self awareness in a social context had been developed by G. H. Mead (1934). Mead placed much more emphasis on the central constructive role of social experience in the development of thinking than Piaget has ever done, and at the same time went further in outlining the detailed processes involved.

Although Mead's theory of mental development has nothing like the degree of articulation and coherence which Piaget has achieved, he sketched the outlines of a theory which is very relevant to present considerations. Mead was not primarily concerned with developmental psychology, and his influence has not been felt until recently in the developmental field, but his writings contain a wealth of suggestions for approaches to developmental phenomena.

Like Wallon, Mead was concerned to attack the long-established individualism of Western philosophy. He tried to free himself from the Cartesian assumption that each individual starts with a knowledge of his own self and works from this towards a knowledge of other selves. Mead attempted to start with social behaviour and to show how 'selfhood' emerged from it. Mead's concept of self is of central importance to the theory, but it is a difficult concept, always in danger of reification. For Mead, self refers to reflexive activity and not to an object or essence.

If we substitute 'self-consciousness' or 'self-awareness' for Mead's term 'self', then we have to distinguish self consciousness from consciousness, or what Mead would simply call 'experience'. He did not want to suggest that the very young child was not aware or conscious in any sense, but that the young child differed from the adult in not being able to 'stand back from' his own direct experience and view it 'from the outside', as it were. Mead saw the development of this sort of meta-awareness as a crucial development, and it was in terms of this concept that he provided the outline at least of a mechanism through which social experience could act back upon the individual child's experience.

The central principle of Mead's theory is that self-consciousness is developed through social interaction, and that one may know oneself only to the extent that one knows others. Mead argued that the isolated, purely individual self is a philosophical fiction, an argument which has been eloquently put in more recent years by John Macmurray (1957).

Mead suggested that the experience of the young child is entirely experience of the outside world, including social 'others'. The child has direct awareness of other people and of what is going on around him, but he cannot become self-aware (aware of his own thoughts and feelings) in the same direct way. He cannot by himself make his thoughts and feelings the objects of his own awareness. Mead's thesis is that such self awareness can only be attained by an individual indirectly, through the mediation of social activity.

The very young child is capable of both intelligent behaviour and emotional responsiveness, but he cannot think about his own reasoning, cannot reflect on his own feelings. Gradually the child's awareness extends to the fact that other people have thoughts, feelings and points of view which may not be identical with his own. He is then able to perceive their reactions to him as reflecting their perspective on him as an object of their social experience, and in this indirect way he brings himself into his own field of experience *as a social object*.

This is first of all achieved with respect to particular other individuals ('significant others'), so that the child's first socially mediated images of himself are gained in close interaction with one or two particular social others, perhaps particularly the parents. In time, the standpoint from which the child views himself becomes relatively generalised and the child constructs an internal 'generalised other' (see Mead, 1934), so that his self awareness is no longer tied to actual interactions with particular others. But without social interaction such self awareness could never have been achieved.†

Self awareness, then, involves awareness of others. Both emerge at the same time; the child becomes an object of his own experience by taking the attitudes of other individuals towards himself within a context of experience and behaviour in which both he and they are involved.

Piaget has described intelligence as 'a process which constructs its own objects'. In these terms Mead's 'self' is an object constructed like any other, except for the difficulty that it only exists experientially insofar as others respond to it. Thus, if intelligence constructs the self-as-object, it does so only in a social context.

For Mead (as to some extent for Wallon) the mechanism whereby the individual becomes able to view himself as an object is that of *role-taking*. The standpoint of others provides 'a platform for getting outside oneself' as Meltzer (1967) puts it, and the development of the self is concurrent with the development of the ability to take roles.

We are here following Sarbin's (1954) distinction between role-taking and role-enactment; role-taking refers to responses made in reference to another person as a social object. Taking the role of the other is a covert,

---

† This notion of a reflexive basis of the sense of self finds fairly frequent expression in more modern writings outside of developmental psychology. For example, R. D. Laing's book *The Self and Others* (*1961*) has as a principal theme the idea that every relationship involves a definition of self by other and a definition of other by self, and that a definition of self by self emerges only gradually out of such relationships. Harré and Secord, in *The Explanation of Social Behaviour* propose that 'unless we can see that other individuals see us as a person, we cannot see ourselves as such' (1972, p. 8).

cognitive process; the ability to 'put oneself in the place of' another person and to make inferences concerning the other's capabilities, attributes, expectations, feelings and potential reactions. Selman provides a clear statement of this definition: 'Following Mead (1934) role-taking is here defined as the tendency to perceive and conceptualise the interaction between oneself and another as seen through the other's eyes. Role-taking is a prototypical social-cognitive skill' (1970, p. 3).

Often, instead of using the expression 'taking the role of the other' Mead substitutes 'entering into the perspective of the other', intending by both these expressions the cognitive process of taking account of another's point of view. The term 'role-taking' is used in preference to 'perspective-taking' in the present volume because it is less loaded in terms of a visual metaphor.

In the process of development, then, the child gradually becomes aware of a diversity of perspectives upon a situation in which he and others are involved. Before this, the young child is not distinguishing between his awareness of, or perspective on, a situation and that situation itself. The development of the ability to role-take permits a differentiation of the observer from the observed – permits the child to be, in a sense, detached from that which he is observing. The implications of this for both cognitive and social behaviour are profound. Effective communication with others not sharing an identical perspective becomes possible, as does flexible and intelligent cooperation with others. The child is able to grasp the perspective of the other, and to modify his own behaviour in the light of that perspective.

Mead emphasised *play* in his account of these developments. Whether play should be regarded as illustrating and reflecting the processes involved or as being itself causally involved is something of a moot point. Mead emphasised that much of the young child's play consists in assuming the roles of a variety of other people (here we are dealing with role-enactment, in Sarbin's sense, rather than role-taking). The prevalence of doll play is interesting in this connection, as are the imaginary companions which some children have. Mead saw the long period of dependence in the human infant as providing ideal conditions for these early stages of the process.

Through transitional forms children move towards organised games, in which one has to take the roles of all the others involved in the common activity; one has to take cognisance of the whole organised activity in order to play one's part successfully. The activity of role-taking is generalised, the child assuming the role of *any* other participating in the game, the roles being specified in the rules of the game. This illustrates Mead's concept of taking the role of the generalised other, which refers to the sharing of perspectives in a transaction.

For Mead, then, a stable and continuous self consciousness is achieved through the generalisation of the perspectives of particular others. Initially the child has a fragmentary identity *vis-à-vis* this or that significant other, but gradually he achieves an identity which is reasonably coherent and continuous. The importance of continuity in the sense of self is that it provides the basis for organising the contents of consciousness. Mead saw the young child as living in an undifferentiated 'now', and as being subject to all the impulses and stimuli directly playing upon him. The older, more self aware child begins to organise these into a flow of experience referent to a self with a fixed past and a more or less uncertain future.†

Mead attributed a critical role to language in the genesis and mediation of reflective conduct. His treatment of 'egocentric speech' as an intermediate form between social and inner speech is very much in line with Vygotsky's view. This is one of the only areas where Mead's views have been systematically compared with Piaget's in the literature (Kohlberg, Yaeger and Hjertholm, 1968). It is perhaps worth quoting from Kohlberg *et al.* a succint statement of that which differentiates Mead from Piaget as regards their ideas on the function of egocentric speech:

> From Piaget's view, the child already has an awareness of the meaning of his action to himself prior to communicating this awareness to others. The child's speech is egocentric if the child ignores either the fact that the auditor already has the awareness of the child's action (i.e. he can see what the child is doing) or the fact that the auditor is not listening to the child's communication of this awareness. From Mead's view, however, the young child does not have an awareness of his own action prior to communicating about it to others. . . When the young child's communication to others is primarily focussed upon eliciting the child's own awareness of the meaning of his action (rather than upon eliciting a response from the other) it appears egocentric [p. 704].

---

† This idea was not new, of course. As far back as 1888 Paul Natorp argued that: 'All conscious experiences have this in common, that. . .their content has. . .reference to a center for which self is the name, in virtue of which reference alone their content is subjectively given' (see James, 1904a).

Mead saw in language the perfect exemplification of a system of 'significant symbols' – symbols which can elicit in the speaker the same response that they elicit in the listener. Berger and Luckmann (1967) discuss at length the way in which a conversation provides one with access to *one's own* subjectivity. In conclusion they quote the saying: 'men must talk about themselves until they know themselves'. Mead argued that reflective thinking followed from an internalisation of such conversations of significant symbols; reflection essentially consists in internalised dialogue. The child comes to be able to signify meanings to himself, and is thereby enabled to direct, control and organise his own behaviour. Behaviour results from a dialogue: the individual initiates action and then responds to that incipient action, taking account of alternative perspectives, and then perhaps revises the course of action in the light of those perspectives. The very quality of thought, then, is seen as reflecting the quality of experienced social interaction.

Mead, Piaget and thinking

Mead's theory suggests that the implications of role-taking extend beyond social behaviour to encompass all aspects of mental development, including those which Flavell (1963) graphically termed 'cold blooded cognition'. The ability to entertain alternative perspectives on a situation makes possible a detachment which is seen by Mead as crucial to intellectual development. We saw earlier that Piaget equated the problem of centering on a particular social perspective with that of centering on a particular aspect of a situation. Mead is here making the same equation, and arguing that social decentration is a necessary condition for intellectual decentration.

The similarity of Mead's and Piaget's ideas on thinking is apparent. The cognitive phenomena which Mead would see as showing the beginnings of 'reflective self awareness' are seen by Piaget as marking the beginnings of what he calls 'reflective abstraction' (e.g. Piaget, 1971). Mead identified the outstanding characteristics of the cognitive processes made possible by role-taking as internalisation and flexibility, with a reversible exchange of meanings. These are, of course, exactly the characteristics stressed in Piaget's account of cognitive development in this period.

Action is central to both theories. It is important to recognise that Mead did not suggest that the child achieves reflective conduct and self awareness by passively internalising the social world. These things are achieved through the action of the subject in the world, via the reponses of others to his action. As a 'pragmatist' Mead was convinced that thinking is rooted in action, and that its role is in devising new plans for action.†

For Piaget, of course, thinking is construed in terms of operations which themselves result from the internalisation of actions. More generally, Piaget's view of the child is as an active, constructive organism, and this seems entirely consistent with Mead's view. The child is not to be conceived as passive in Mead's theorising, any more than in Piaget's. On the one hand man is social, on the other hand he is not simply socially determined. The individual acts in terms of his knowledge of himself, and one may provide a sociogenic account of that knowledge and of how it mediates the individual's action. Nonetheless action remains in the last resort the prerogative of the individual, the self-as-actor, rather than of the socially determined image of the self. Mead emphasised that the child is from birth an actor as well as a reactor. He does not simply respond to stimuli outside himself, and indeed the effective nature of the stimulus is dependent upon the individual and the activity in which the individual is engaged (Miller, 1973). Within the Meadian tradition, the environment is thought of as being 'a selected segment of the "real" world, the selection occurring in the interests of behaviour which the human being himself has initiated' (Stryker, 1967, p. 373). This conception is, of course, directly compatible with Piaget's notion of assimilation.

Mead gave central significance to thinking in his account of development, and saw the self as essentially a cognitive rather than an emotional phenomenon. Here again Mead and Piaget tend to agree, when contrasted with the positions of Cooley, James and especially Wallon on this point. Wallon argued that the emotions could be considered as the origin of consciousness, and this contributed to the antagonistic exchanges between Wallon and Piaget (Voyat, 1973).

There are thus considerable similarities between Mead's views and Piaget's. Indeed, if we examine Piaget's writings over the years we find most of Mead's arguments implicity acknowledged. As noted earlier, Piaget has recognised that the concept of egocentrism has profound implications for the child's self-awareness or self-knowledge, and the idea of mentality as dialogue also occurs in Piaget's early writings: 'Logical reasoning is an argument which we have with ourselves, and which

† William James put this position particularly clearly: 'Beliefs are really rules for action, and the whole function of thinking is but one step in the production of...action' (James, 1904b, p. 673).

reproduces internally the features of a real argument.' (Piaget, 1928, p. 204.)

However, Piaget's ground has shifted over the years, as we remarked in an earlier section. Increasingly, developments in the interpersonal sphere have come to be seen as mere epiphenomena, reflecting the underlying processes of individual cognition. While he pays lip service to the idea that the development of reflective thought is an essentially social process, it is no longer clear how, if at all, social experience qualitatively affects that development. It is here that Mead's views stand in marked contrast to Piaget's.

It may be felt that all that is at issue here is the choice of one research area rather than another to concentrate upon. Mead has chosen to focus upon the dialectic between the developing individual and society, while Piaget has focussed upon the dialectic between the developing child and the nonsocial environment. However, if we take the theories of Vygotsky, Wallon or especially Mead seriously, we must realise that these two aspects of development are not separable, they are not even simply parallel, but rather they are inextricably interrelated. Piaget asserts that the tendency of the egocentric child to center on one feature of a situation leads to serious distortions in his reasoning. We may apply just this argument to Piaget's own work, and conclude that his tendency to center upon the individual must distort his theory of intellectual development. Perhaps more consideration by developmental psychologists of the work of G. H., Mead may aid the necessary process of decentration. If, in Piaget's own words 'logical thought is necessarily social' (1950, p. 165), then no theory can be coherent, let alone adequate, if it fails to consider the significance of the social other for the development of the child's thought.

Research approaches

Mead's theory contains clear suggestions as to which aspects of the child's development in the preschool period should repay further study. Communication (especially through speech), private or 'egocentric' speech, role playing, rule games and role-taking are all seen to be of great interest. As noted earlier, egocentric speech is one of the only topics to have been examined empirically from the point of view of a comparison of Mead's position with that of Piaget. Kohlberg, Yaeger and Hjertholm (1968) developed differential predictions from Piaget, Mead and Vygotsky regarding the course of development of egocentric speech, Vygotsky's position being very close to Mead's. These included predictions about the prevalence of such speech at different ages, the relationship of prevalence of egocentric speech to a measure of intelligence, and the qualitative characteristics of such speech. 'Inner speech' would be expected to develop characteristics, such as condensation and omission of the referent, which would make it progressively less and less like social speech. Their findings from a number of observational studies were largely consistent with predictions drawn from Vygotsky and Mead, leading them to the conclusion that the various forms of private speech represent different developmental levels of behaviour with a common self communicative functional significance.†

The details of their studies need not be pursued here, but they illustrate some important points. On the one hand they show something of the potential relevance of Mead's ideas to detailed developmental issues. On the other hand they illustrate the difficulties of finding and testing specific differential predictions from theoretical positions on the level of generality of Piaget's or Mead's. Even where, as in this case, particular predictions can be drawn reasonably unambiguously from the theories, the outcome is not necessarily decisive. Mead does not provide anything like a complete alternative to Piaget's theory. Kohlberg *et al.*'s study of egocentric speech clearly does not provide a basis for rejecting Piaget's ideas on egocentrism *in toto*, nor does it make clear what must be rejected and what retained.

A more eclectic research strategy seems sensible in this area, and has been adopted in the present study. Role-taking, in the sense defined earlier, has been selected as a topic which is pertinent to central issues in the several theoretical positions described. Mead's theory obviously suggests that studies of the role-taking process should be rewarding, but until very recently there has been little work done on this, especially with preschool children. Moreover, Piaget's view of the relevant developmental processes is in many ways similar to Mead's, and could by itself provide the basis and justification of the role-taking process. Flavell (1968) makes this point in a quotation which also provides a useful summary of this chapter:

> Piaget...asserted that a fundamental and pervasive quality of the young child's thought is it's egocentrism, consisting of a general incognizance of the notion of 'points of view' and hence a lack of

† Some of the findings of the Kohlberg study, for instance of more private speech amongst brighter than amongst average IQ children at certain ages, have been confirmed by Deutch and Stein (1972). On the other hand Rubin, Hultsch and Peters (1971) found Kohlberg's *qualitative* hierarchy of types of private speech, less reliable and less sequential than one might wish.

awareness of how the child's own may differ from other people's. His cognitive field of vision includes the data thought about, but not the process of thinking itself. Insensitive to the very fact that the way he construes the data is only one construction among many possible (because the construing process itself never becomes an object of thought), it follows that he can scarcely check for cognitive bias in his own view of events, can scarcely enquire about the difference between this and other views, and so on. *Thus intellectual egocentrism is fundamentally an inability to take roles* [pp. 16/17, my emphasis]

The broad theoretical approaches outlined in this chapter will be considered again later in the light of our research findings. However, the primary aim of this study is not so much to test the relative merits of these approaches as to extend our present rather meagre knowledge concerning role-taking. If role-taking is really the 'prototypical social-cognitive skill', then it ought to be possible in a study of role-taking to discern at least some of the ways in which individual and social aspects of thinking interact in the process of development.

2

Putting yourself in somebody else's shoes

In this chapter a number of empirical approaches to the study and measurement of role-taking will be described, beginning with Piaget and Inhelder's (1956) study of visual perspective taking. We shall briefly examine more recent work on this topic, and then extend consideration to the wide variety of other studies which have developed and elaborated the idea of role-taking. This will lead to a discussion of the available evidence regarding conditions which favour or impede the development of the child's role-taking ability. The review will necessarily be somewhat selective, picking out issues which will be of relevance in later chapters. Shantz (1975) provides a more general review of the available literature on the development of 'social cognition'.

The coordination of visual perspectives
We have seen that Piaget regards the processes of intellectual and social 'decentering' as merely two aspects of the same development. Intellectual and social egocentrism decline simultaneously as the child grows out of the pre-operatory stage. Moreover Piaget considers that this decline may be indexed by the child's success or failure on tasks requiring consideration of perspectives in the visual, perceptual sense. His paradigmatic study (Piaget and Inhelder, 1956) is concerned with the ability to work out what another person can see. Flavell's (1968) studies with preschool children show a similar bias, and he suggests that young children might be expected to grasp perceptual perspective differences before being able to deal with perspectives involving cognitions, emotions, motives etc.

Piaget and Inhelder (1956) reported a number of studies of the 'spatial' aspect of egocentrism – the coordination of visual perspectives.

One of them, the 'Doll and Mountains' experiment, has since been regarded almost as an operational definition of spatial egocentrism. Children were presented with a 3D model of three mountains and were asked to identify the perspective of a doll which occupied different viewing positions from that of the child himself. The child had to respond either by arranging three pieces of cardboard to represent a view of the three mountains or by choosing amongst ten pictures. A variant involved the child having to place the doll in a position corresponding to a given picture. Three stages were distinguished by Piaget and Inhelder. In the first (between approximately 4 and 7 years) the children responded in an egocentric manner, tending to attribute their own perspective to the doll. Seven and eight year olds were in a transitional stage where errors were made which were not predominantly egocentric. Not until 9 or 10 years of age did children perform without errors. In the first stage, then, it seemed that children lacked the knowledge that the appearance of objects is a function of the spatial position from which they are viewed. In the second stage they have this knowledge, but only in the third stage do they acquire the ability to determine what that appearance would be for any specific viewing position.

Piaget and Inhelder conducted this study as part of a more extensive investigation of the development of spatial frameworks. A number of the more recent studies share this primary concern with the construction by the child of a projective representation of space (e.g. Coie, Costanzo and Farnhill, 1973; Nigl and Fishbein, 1974, Pufall, 1975). Shantz (1975) makes the point of her review that such studies may tell us more about the child's emerging spatial representation than about role-taking. Following Fishbein (Nigl and Fishbein, 1974) we can perhaps usefully distinguish between social and conceptual aspects of perspective-taking tasks. Conceptual aspects concern the inferences involved in the construction of the other's view, while the social aspect is represented by the tendency for the child to select his own view, acting as though the instruction made reference to himself rather than to another. Given such a distinction, our present concerns are primarily with the social aspect of these tasks – with their use as indices of social egocentrism.

Returning to the 'Doll and Mountains' task, then, we may agree that correct solution of such a task requires complex spatial transformations which appear to be well beyond the cognitive capacities of preschool children. But the finding that the younger children's errors were predominantly egocentric is an essentially separate one, since in the transitional stage children were typically wrong without being egocentric. Piaget and Inhelder said of the child in the first stage that he: 'appears to be rooted to his own viewpoint in the narrowest and most restrictive fashion so that he cannot imagine any perspective but his own' (1956, p. 242). If this is taken to imply that the child up to the age of about seven years will respond egocentrically regardless of the task, then it is a conclusion which has been seriously undermined by more recent studies. The relationship of task difficulty to egocentric responding is a complex one (see, for example, Salatas and Flavell, 1976) but the recent literature certainly suggests that the ability to coordinate visual perspectives is a function of the particular task presented, and that in some circumstances nonegocentric responses may be elicited as early as the second or third year of life.

Fishbein, Lewis and Keiffer (1972) refer to a study in which children were asked to choose a photograph which showed the experimenter's perspective on a single toy. They found that even $3\frac{1}{2}$ year olds performed quite well on this task, the majority of errors being egocentric. It may be that replacing the doll with a real observer helped (cf. Cox, 1975), or it may be that the high level of performance followed from the fact that the children only had to deal with one object. Fishbein, Lewis and Keiffer (1972) conducted another study in which they used an array of toys. In one condition (the 'turning' task) the child had to rotate the table so that the experimenter could view the toys from a specified perspective. The other condition ('pointing') resembled the previous study – the child had to point to a photograph depicting what the experimenter could see. There was a great difference in the level of performance in the two conditions. Even the youngest children ($3\frac{1}{2}$ years) had little difficulty with the turning task but the pointing task proved quite difficult, the level of difficulty depending on the number of toys in the array. Hoy (1974) reports similar studies, concluding that: 'Children's ability to reproduce another's view is dependent on the type and number of dimensions which must be considered simultaneously and on the type of response required' (p. 462).

Shantz and Watson (1971) used a task similar to the 'Doll and Mountains' task together with another in which the child himself moved and had to predict the view from his new position, the objects being covered during the move. With $3\frac{1}{2}$–$6\frac{1}{2}$ year old children the former task proved very difficult but the latter unexpectedly easy. They suggest that in the former task the visible presence of the child's own view may make it harder for him to detach himself from it in order to appreciate the other's. They found that if the easier task was done first, it facilitated performance on the 'Doll and Mountain' type of task. Huttenlocher and Presson (1973) obtained similar results to those of Shantz and Watson on a task in which the child himself moved and had to predict his new view. They also found that tasks in which the child had to anticipate the appearance of an array of objects which was rotated were very much easier for young children than tasks in which the child had to anticipate the appearance of a fixed array to an observer who moved around it.

Moving ever further down the age scale, a group of studies by Masangkay, McCluskey, McIntyre, Simms-Knight, Vaughan and Flavell (1974) demonstrated the capacity for some basic inferences about visual perspective in children as young as $2\frac{1}{2}$–3 years. For example, the child at this age can understand that when a card with a different picture on each side is interposed between himself and another person, that person can see the picture which he himself cannot see. In a recently published study Lempers, Flavell and Flavell (1977) investigated pointing, showing and hiding behaviours of children aged 1–3 years. Even these children showed considerable evidence of effective accommodation to another's viewpoint.†

For present purposes, all that is important is to recognise that from early infancy the child appears to show some sensitivity to alternative visual perspectives, but that such sensitivity will probably only be manifest in very simple situations where the instructions are explicit and the content of the perspectives uncomplicated. Development from this point onwards is towards a greater disposition to take perspectives and a greater ability to construct the content of another's perspective, so that perspective taking becomes manifest in more, and in more complex, situations. We are suggesting, then, a gradual development of perspective-taking abilities which has already begun by the second or third year of life and which is quite well advanced by the end of the preschool period.

Other approaches

All the studies considered thus far have concerned the ability of the child *literally* to see somebody else's point of view. But the expression 'point

† To study role-taking at still earlier stages of infancy it is obvious that different research techniques are required. It may be, for example, that recent studies of the infant's capacity to establish joint visual regard with the mother (Scaife and Bruner, 1975; Butterworth and Cochran, 1978) should be seen as indications of an early recognition of the other's point of view.

of view' has a much wider metaphorical usage, and the notion of role-taking as it emerged in the first chapter encompasses these wider meanings. All situations which depend upon the child recognising and accommodating to the thoughts, feelings and intentions (as well as the percepts) of another person can be said to involve role-taking.

John Flavell (1968) conducted a wide ranging study of role-taking in middle childhood and adolescence, providing valuable descriptions of the nature and patterns of acquisition of various abilities subsumed under the heading of role-taking. In his tasks, wherever possible the role attributes of the 'subject' and those of the 'object' of role-taking were made as distinct as possible; in most cases the roles were opposite or complementary in some sense. He divided the tasks used into two types: those involving a straightforward inference which might be correct or incorrect, and those in which there is no 'right answer', but where the interest is in the degree of subtlety of the child's role-taking in the situation. The latter category covers all social guessing games which involve the potentially infinite chain of inference: 'I think that he's thinking that I'm thinking...'. For example Flavell used a 'nickel and dime' game: two cups were inverted and a coin placed under each. The cups were marked with the value of the coin placed under them. While one of the observers went out of the room, the other instructed the child to remove one of the coins – whichever one he liked. The other observer returned and had to choose a cup; if he chose the one which still had a coin under it he 'won' the money. Most of the youngest children tested by Flavell (7–8 year olds) took out the larger coin and voiced the expectation that the other would go for that one 'because it's more'. The next step involves the realisation by the child that his own cognitions can be included in the other's cognitive field – in other words that the observer may guess that the child will take the larger coin away and will therefore choose the smaller, and so on.

De Vries (1970) and Berner (1971) approached this recursive property of thinking using a technique more applicable to preschool children. The child was simply told to 'guess which hand the penny is in' as the experimenter's hands were repeatedly hidden behind his back and closed fists presented to the child. Then in a further series of trials the child was asked to hide the penny for the experimenter to make guesses. De Vries' results with 3–6 year old children suggested a five stage sequence of development from a total lack of recognition of the need for secrecy and deceptiveness in the first stage to a fifth stage in which the child was competitive and attempted to outwit the experimenter by using an irregular, shifting strategy. The appearance of competitive and deceptive hiding prior to competitive and deceptive guessing suggested that the child was able to take account of the other's taking account of his perspective. Berner obtained essentially similar results.

Most of the tasks Flavell (1968) used fell into the category in which there was a 'right answer' and where interest centered upon specific errors or failures of role-taking. For example, he used a picture story composed of seven pictures. When the child had 'told' the story depicted, three of the pictures were removed. The sequence was so constructed that the remaining four pictures still made a meaningful story, but one which was significantly different from the original. The youngest children (seven year olds) all grasped the original 7-picture story and could express it easily. But for the 4-picture story varying degrees of contamination from the original story were evident in the stories of most of the seven year olds. Success on this task requires the child to allow for the possibility of a number of different constructions being put upon a picture, depending on its context. The child whose perception of the four pictures remains distorted by his interpretation of the seven is thus showing an inability to 'decenter' in Piaget's sense.

Chandler (1972) used a closely related procedure, involving a series of 12 cartoon sequences. Each time the child was required to tell the story shown in the sequence, and then to retell it from the point of view of one of the characters in the story. The stories were designed to include certain 'privileged' information, available to the reader but not to the story character whose perspective he had to adopt. The unwarranted inclusion of such privileged information in the second account was taken as evidence of a deficiency in role-taking.

The measures described so far have very largely omitted the affective side of role-taking: sensitivity to the emotional attributes of others. Borke (1971, 1973) approached this problem by presenting children between 3 and 8 years of age with a series of short stories. They were asked to indicate how the child in each situation felt by selecting a 'happy', 'sad', 'afraid' or 'angry' face to complete the picture accompanying each story. Children as young as 3 years appeared to show an awareness of other people's feelings and could identify the specific situations which evoke different kinds of emotional responses. This applied particularly to the 'happy' sentiment, which was used almost perfectly by the youngest children. Borke suggested that the surprisingly good performance of the preschool children on this task resulted from the fact that it required behavioural rather than verbal responses.

Chandler and Greenspan (1972) have argued that Borke's task is not a valid test of role-taking, on the grounds that the child is merely generating stereotyped responses on the basis of projecting himself into the situations described in the stories. Selman (1973) has defined role-taking as understanding the nature of the relation between the self's and other's perspectives. Chandler and Greenspan argue that this *relationship* of perspectives can only be tested in situations which demand a clear differentiation of one's own perspective from that of the other person. They cite the Chandler picture story test, described earlier, as being criterial of a valid test, since it involves a conflict between what the *reader* knows about how character *A* is feeling and what another story character *B* knows about *A*'s feelings.† A recent study by Mossler, Marvin and Greenberg (1976) employed an adaptation of Flavell's picture story technique, greatly simplifying it. They used videotaped presentation followed by questions demanding yes or no answers, and concluded that four to five year old children were able to engage in 'veridical perspective taking' even in a task containing demonstrably different perspectives. Doubtless much more work will have to be done in this area before consensus is achieved. The abilities which Borke demonstrates must surely underlie later developments, and she is perhaps justified in commenting (1972) that we should spend less time arguing about the age at which 'true' role-taking can be demonstrated, and more time looking at the factors affecting the emergence of relevant processes in early childhood.

Flavell (1968) also investigated communicational aspects of role-taking, arguing that effective communication depends upon the child taking an accurate measure of the listener's role attributes and then actively using this knowledge to shape and adapt his message accordingly. In one task the child was asked to give instructions to another who was blindfolded, to see whether he adapted the content of his messages accordingly. In another task the child had to tell a story to a pictured four year old and then to a pictured adult. In another, the child had to detect the inadequacies of a message constructed by the experimenter (who had

---

† Chandler and Greenspan's position is clearly in the tradition of many of Piaget's concrete operations tasks, which are set up in such a way that there is an inherent conflict, between the perceptually compelling preoperational solution on the one hand and the 'correct' operational solution on the other.

a map) for the guidance of a fictional character who was lost. Flavell remarks that even the youngest children showed considerable competence on such tasks. However, some of the tasks used were very complex. For example, the problem of the police chief and the combination lock (1968, p. 118) involves multiple listeners all possessing different subsets of the total set of information. Such a task may be insoluble by younger children because of their inability to handle the complex coordinations involved.

Again we face the problem that when a child fails on a task it is often difficult to decide whether the child does not know that others have different viewpoints (existence), or whether he is unaware that this is a task which requires this knowledge (need) or whether he is simply finding difficulty in working out the other's perspective (application). The 'need' component perhaps deserves more attention than it has generally received. Flavell remarks that: 'Whatever the underlying cause, the net effect is a marked gap between our hypothetical child's developed *capabilities* for social cognition and the amount of social cognition he *spontaneously carries out*' (1974, p. 76).

Flavell uses the following example: a child of six or more might quite typically say 'you put that thing in the cup' when explaining something to a listener who, being blindfolded or behind a screen, cannot see the object to which the child is referring. In interpreting this 'egocentric communication failure' it would presumably be wrong to suppose that the child actively believes that his listener *can* see, and presumably also wrong to suppose that he considers his message to be adequate to a listener who *cannot* see. It seems rather that he fails to pay attention to this listener and thus fails to see the need to adapt his messages to his listener's needs.

An apparent disparity between underlying abilities and actual performance has been noted in other studies. Levine and Hoffman (1975), in their study of empathy in four year olds, point to a marked gap between the availability of inferential skills and the use made of them. Acredolo (1977) suggests that the period around four years of age may be one in which the gap between the ability to coordinate perspectives and the spontaneous use of such ability is particularly wide. She makes this suggestion on the basis of a study in which prompts and reminders were found to be uniquely effective in improving performance at this age. We shall return to this question in later chapters.

The general picture which emerges from the studies reviewed thus far is that some basic forms of role-taking emerge very early in childhood but that they are initially fragile, situation specific, and heavily dependent upon contextual and instructional cues. Such a picture is consistent with direct observational studies of young children. If the preschool child were really wholly unable to imagine any perspective other than his own, as Piaget and Inhelder (1956) seem to suggest, then genuine social behaviour, especially cooperative behaviour, should be absent. But a number of studies (e.g. Swift, 1964) have shown cooperative play to be well established by four years of age. Similarly Mueller (1972) questions the assumption that spontaneous verbal interaction amongst preschool children is limited as a result of egocentrism. His study of four year olds in free play indicates that on the contrary the children almost always displayed social interest and usually received replies to the things they said. They were surprisingly competent in various aspects of social communication. Garvey and Hogan (1973) reinforce this finding: in their study of 3½–5 year olds they found a high level of mutual responsiveness in both speech and behaviour. Amongst other studies suggesting quite subtle social judgement in the preschool period are those of Maratsos (1973) and Shatz and Gelman (1973). Known features of the behaviour of preschool children thus lend some weight to the findings of the role-taking studies which have been reviewed. Such children undoubtedly do behave egocentrically in a host of ways, but their egocentrism is far from complete and does not constitute nearly as tight a strait-jacket as has often been supposed.

Individual differences and their generality
In Flavell's (1968) studies of role-taking he repeatedly observed a very wide range of individual differences between children of the same age. Other authors (e.g. Hughes, 1975) have made the same observations – where several age groups are studied the individual variation within one age group may be very large relative to the differences between age groups. Such individual differences raise a number of interesting questions, the first of which concerns their generality. We have mentioned in this chapter a wide range of possible approaches to the measurement of role-taking skills. If we can speak of role-taking as a *general* skill (or disposition) then individual differences should be reasonably stable across a range of tasks. Put simply, if we give a number of tasks all supposedly tapping role-taking skills to the same children, will the children who are good at one of them be good at all of them?

Shantz and Watson's (1971) finding of a significant relationship between the number of errors made by individual children on their two tasks (see p. 19), despite their widely differing difficulty levels, suggests a degree of generalisability of individual differences across tasks. Rubin (1973) has examined patterns of performance of 5–11 year olds across a range of tasks. He included a measure of egocentric or private speech, a measure of spatial egocentrism, a measure of recursiveness of thinking and a measure of communicational accuracy. Analysis indicated a cluster of substantial intercorrelations between these tasks, with the exception of the private speech measures. A principal components analysis yielded further support in the form of a first factor accounting for over fifty per cent of the variance on which the role-taking tasks (excepting private speech) all loaded heavily. The results for private speech may be seen as supporting the interpretation put on this phenomenon by Vygotsky and by Mead (see Ch. 1).

Hollos and Cowan (1973; Hollos, 1975) administered a version of the Doll and Mountains task, Flavell's picture story task and a communicational accuracy task to 7–9 year old children in Norway and subsequently in Hungary. They also gave the same children a range of logical operations tasks. Their results seemed to give some confirmation of the statistical unitariness of the role-taking measures. A principal components analysis of all the scores suggested two interpretable components, one which was strongly associated with the role-taking tasks. The communicational accuracy task was the only one of the 'role-taking group' which loaded heavily on the factor associated with logical operations.†

A study by Van Lieshout, Leckie and Smits-Van Sonsbeek (1973) also found significant intercorrelations between eight out of nine role-taking tasks administered to 3 to 5 year olds, with one major factor on which all eight tasks loaded emerging from the factor analysis. Not all studies have suggested a unitary role-taking factor. Urberg and Docherty (1976) gave five affective role-taking tasks to 3–6 year olds and identified two clusters: the three tasks requiring sequential perspective-taking forming one group and the two requiring simultaneous coordination of perspectives forming another. Kurdek and Rodgon (1975) showed complex age- and sex-dependent relationships between three tasks supposedly tapping role-taking.

Shantz (1975) reviews a number of other studies, mostly unpublished, which bear on this question. Some have quite failed to find significant intercorrelations, although Shantz points out that low correlations might

---

† There are a number of studies which suggest that communicational accuracy is not simply a function of social role-taking (e.g. Coie and Dorval, 1973; Piché *et al.*, 1975).

be artefacts due to poor reliability, limitations of scoring, or variable difficulty levels. She concludes that while some studies have shown 'unexpectedly high' levels of correlation, the overall picture is of only moderate relationships amongst various role-taking skills.

The origins of individual differences

The question of causal interdependencies between social and non-social aspects of cognition was discussed in the previous chapter in relation to the theories of Piaget and Mead. For Mead it was clear that social experience had a determining effect upon general cognitive development and that this effect was mediated by social role-taking. It should, therefore, be possible to show systematic relationships between the development of role-taking and the quality of experienced social inter-actions. Piaget's position is more equivocal: role-taking is seen both as reflecting, and as being reflected in, other aspects of cognitive develop-ment. But in eschewing simple causal models Piaget is not denying that role-taking is potentially susceptible to the influence of specific kinds of social experience.

In his discussions of how egocentrism is overcome, Piaget has placed primary emphasis upon the child's interactions with his peers (see Ch. 1, p. 8). He argues that the social relation of reciprocity, which he sees as crucial, arises between individuals considering themselves as equals. Flavell (1968) suggests that the influence of peer group participation may be better conceptualised as providing general role-taking opportunities than as having very specific or unique forms of influence. He emphasises the possible importance of interactions with certain non-peers, including adults and younger children. He suggests, for instance, that the child who has a somewhat younger sibling may well have particularly good opportunities to stretch his role-taking capabilities. Kohlberg (1969), discussing moral judgement as a special aspect of the development of role-taking, further plays down the importance of the peer group, concluding that the limited evidence available does not support the idea that participation in the peer group plays any critical or unique role in moral development.

Hollos and Cowan's studies in Norway and Hungary were mentioned in the previous section. They studied logical operations and role-taking abilities in children living in towns, in small villages, and in isolated farms. Opportunity for peer interaction decreased from the towns to the farms. They found little effect of social setting upon logical operations (if anything the isolated farm children were superior) and age effects were prominent. But with role-taking the social setting effects predominated, the socially isolated farm children performing very poorly compared to town and village children. However, there was no difference between the latter groups despite the town children having more experience of social interaction. Hollos and Cowan suggest a 'threshold model', in which a minimum of social interaction is a necessary prerequisite of role-taking development, but beyond this level more opportunity for interaction has little effect. West (1974) working in various communities in Israel (city, moshav, kibbutz) found no differences in role-taking, which she interpreted as indicating that all three groups were 'above threshold'. More recently Nahir and Yussen (1977) have shown differences favouring kibbutz children compared to city children on measures of communicative role-taking, which they interpret in terms of the higher level of peer interactions in the kibbutz. They acknowledge, however, that their communication measures may not be at all 'pure' as measures of decentering.

Both Flavell and Kohlberg suggest that participation in social interaction in the home probably provides the major setting for role-taking opportunities, but they give little guidance as to the types of home which might foster role-taking ability. The finding that 'inductive' styles of parental discipline are associated with advanced moral development in the child (Hoffman, 1970) is perhaps relevant, given the association between moral judgement and role-taking (e.g. Ambron and Irwin, 1975). 'Inductive' control involves the giving of reasons and the pointing out of consequences. Shantz (1975) remarks that the parent's verbal explicitness about his own and other people's responses to the child's behaviour bears an almost 'face valid' relationship to the development of the child's role-taking ability. At the other extreme, punishment-oriented discipline is associated with poor moral development, and Piaget has himself suggested that social systems based on authority may hinder the process of decentration (Piaget, 1970).

Basil Bernstein's distinction between 'personal' and 'positional' modes of relation within the family seems to provide a means of clarifying the issues involved here. Bernstein has argued for a close relationship between linguistic codes, role-taking, and the prevailing character of the role relationships:

> An elaborated code encourages the speaker to focus upon the experience of others, as different from his own. In the case of a

restricted code, what is transmitted verbally usually refers to the other person in terms of common group or status membership...
Thus restricted codes could be considered status or positional codes whereas elaborated codes are oriented to persons [1970, p. 476].

Bernstein, acknowledging his indebtedness to Mead, sees the origins of different linguistic codes in the role structure of the family, influencing the child particularly through the means of social control employed. He suggests that in a 'person-oriented' family the child's developing self is differentiated by continuous adjustment to the verbally realised intentions and motives of others. In the positional family the child responds to status requirements, learning a communalised as opposed to an individualised role.

Bernstein and Cook (1968) developed a coding frame dealing with distinctions between various forms of verbal control, utilised subsequently by Brandis and Henderson (1970) and Cook-Gumperz (1973). Some evidence of the relationship between such measures of family interaction and the child's role-taking abilities has been provided by Bearison and Cassel (1975). Children from predominantly person-oriented families showed greater evidence of accommodating their communication to a blindfolded as opposed to a sighted listener than children from predominantly position-oriented families. This issue will be taken up in more detail in chapter 5.

Bernstein's work provides a clear indication of the great variation in the elaboration of verbal expression amongst adults, and Flavell (1968) discusses evidence of stable differences in *adult* role-taking abilities. Robert Hess and his colleagues in Chicago taught simple tasks to mothers of preschool children and then observed the attempts of the mothers to teach these tasks to their children (Hess and Shipman, 1965; Brophy, 1970). The mother–child interchanges evidenced great variability in the extent to which the mother was able to take the perspective of the child on the task. This procedure, then, provides a possible way of getting at relevant aspects of the interaction between mother and child, and is again something to which we shall return in a later chapter (Ch. 5).

Before leaving the question of role-taking opportunities we should note that these may not always take the form of actual social exchanges. It may be that the overt or covert playing out of roles in solitary play is also significant (Mead, 1934). The child may not only practice adult roles, but also role-taking activities like those involved in competitive or cooperative situations. He may rehearse past or future interactions with others, imagining the responses of another occupying a complementary role. In these respects solitary play may provide an important context for role-taking development.

Role-taking and social behaviour

The ability to take the role of another is basic to the ability to comprehend and predict the other's behaviour, so that role-taking can be seen as a prerequisite for many types of social behaviour (Hartup, 1970). This being so, it is natural to consider how individual differences in role-taking are related to individual differences in social behaviour. Available evidence is confusing and conflicting, perhaps partly because few of the studies have used a sufficiently wide variety either of role-taking tasks or of indices of social behaviour.

Zahn-Waxler, Radke-Yarrow and Brady-Smith (1977) did use a battery of role-taking measures but did not find scores to be predictive of 'prosocial interventions' (comforting, helping and sharing) made by 3 to 7 year olds. Jennings (1975) likewise failed to show a relationship between role-taking and observational measures of preference for interaction with people as opposed to objects. However, Jennings' role-taking measures did show positive relationships with ratings of popularity,† peer leadership, and other aspects of social competence. Rothenberg (1970) found an affective role-taking measure to be positively related to peer and teacher ratings of leadership, gregariousness and friendship in 8 to 10 year olds.

As to cooperation, Levine and Hoffman (1975) were unable to show a relationship between affective role-taking and cooperative behaviour in four year olds, though they point to some evidence of such a relationship at later ages. Johnson (1975) did find significant relationships between affective role-taking and cooperation in eleven year olds.

Available evidence on the relationship of role-taking abilities and social adjustment in normal children is thus fairly equivocal. The same can be said of attempts to show effects on cooperative or altruistic behaviour by training normal children in social role-taking skills. Some success has been claimed (e.g. Staub, 1971) but other large-scale and careful studies such as that of Wentink and colleagues (1975) in Holland have failed to show any substantial effects. The evidence from studies of seriously maladjusted children is perhaps more convincing. Neale, in 1966, found

† Studies of the relationship between popularity and role-taking have shown a variety of outcomes (e.g. Rubin, 1973; Deutch, 1974; Gottman, Gonso and Rasmussen, 1975).

that emotionally disturbed, agressive children tended to show very poor role-taking skills. Chandler (1972, 1973) has extended this line of enquiry, using chronically delinquent and emotionally disturbed boys. Using the picture story technique described earlier, he found that, with some exceptions, the disturbed or delinquent children were markedly deficient in role-taking. The typical disturbed child of 13 remained more egocentric than 7 year olds in a control group matched for socioeconomic and ethnic background.† Chandler ran an 'actors workshop' for a group of delinquent children, making extensive use of videotape etc., and claimed to show a significant improvement in role-taking abilities even when compared to another group who were involved in the making of documentary films. Eighteen month follow-ups showed significant reductions in known delinquent behaviour, though Chandler observes that their improved social skills may be reflected in being better able to avoid being caught! Chandler, Greenspan and Barenboim (1974) have also carried out a 12 month follow-up of the effects of training institutionalised emotionally disturbed children in role-taking and communication skills, and found evidence of improvements in social adjustment.

To summarise, then, there is limited and somewhat conflicting evidence as to the existence of a positive relationship between role-taking and social competence in normal young children. There seems to be rather better evidence, at least for older children, of a negative relationship between role-taking and seriously disturbed or antisocial behaviour.

In this chapter we have considered a wide range of empirical evidence relating to the development of role-taking. There seems clear evidence of a capacity for role-taking in a variety of contexts in the preschool period, and some evidence that individual differences are consistent across varying tasks. This consistency, such as it is, may be mediated more by a generalised sensitivity to the *need* to take the other's point of view than by any generalised skills or inferences required in order to be *able* to do so.

Flavell commented in 1968 that: 'It can now be taken as a fact that...the developmental *rate* of skill acquisition in this area is enormously variable from child to child' (p. 218). He went on to add that 'We should

---

† It is interesting in this connection to recall the early work of John Bowlby (1946) on 'affectionless character' in delinquents. He related this to deprivation of mother-love in early childhood. Chandler's study seems to equate affectionless character development with an inability to empathise or role-take, which may indeed have its origins in early social relationships.

like to know just what qualities or characteristics of the individual and of his environment during the formative years contribute to or impede the attainment of these skills' (p. 220). In the preceding pages we have drawn together a variety of suggestions and a small body of evidence concerning the antecedents and consequences of well- and poorly-developed role-taking abilities. But no very adequate answers are available to the questions which Flavell raises, and it is to these questions that the research reported in the following chapters is addressed. The principal justification for searching for the social-interactional antecedents of role-taking skill must be in terms of developmental theory. The possibilities of a link between poor role-taking and disturbed or antisocial behaviour provide an alternative and more practical justification for such a study.

3

Role-taking: problems and games

Introduction: the children

Before entering into detailed descriptions of the measures of role-taking ability used in the present study some background information will be given on the children who participated in the research. The children's parents had been recruited to a longitudinal study sample just prior to the birth of the child. Martin Richards and Judy Dunn (Bernal) recruited seventy-seven families for the purpose of an intensive study of the first sixty weeks of the child's life. Their work was financed by a grant from the Nuffield Foundation. The sample consisted of first- and second-born children of British born parents resident within the city of Cambridge. Pregnancy and delivery had to be normal, as determined by a wide variety of criteria derived mainly from Butler and Bonham (1963). Families were recruited to the sample via midwives, and some degree of selection undoubtedly occurred at this level. A combination of these factors led to an under-representation in the sample of the lower end of the social class spectrum, although many manual workers' families were included. Of the families suggested by the midwives, very few were unwilling to cooperate, and surprisingly few have dropped out since, considering the demands that have been made upon them. This point will be taken up in more detail a little later.

The research effort over the first sixty weeks of the child's life was directed towards detailed observation of the interaction of mother and child. One of the foci has been the influence of newborn characteristics upon the pattern of interaction during the first year, especially in connection with feeding, sleeping and crying. Another concern has been the influence of obstetric medication upon mother–infant interaction.

During this early work a good deal of background sociological and demographic information was collected. Frances Barnes saw the children at the age of 3 years in the course of a separate research project financed by the Mental Health Research Fund. She was concerned on the one hand with how far information about pregnancy and the child's state at delivery is predictive of his development over the first few years, and on the other hand with an observational study of communicational interactions between the mothers and their children.

The Nuffield Foundation extended the original grant in order that further follow-up studies might be undertaken, and the present author was principally responsible for research carried out when the children reached four years of age. Further data were collected when the children reached school age, the work being supported in part by a grant from the Social Science Research Council. In chapter 6, aspects of the earlier and later work will be discussed in more detail, but chapters 3, 4 and 5 are based on the study of the children at four years of age.

All children were seen and tested between the ages of 4 years 0 months and 4 years 1 month, giving an exceptionally narrow age range. The sample at this stage consisted of sixty children, 28 boys and 32 girls. Losses from the original sample were mainly due to families moving either abroad or too far away for us to continue seeing them. Families who moved away from Cambridge but remained within about 100 mile radius were not dropped from the sample. This entailed a considerable amount of travelling but was undertaken in order to avoid too great a bias arising from the loss of the more mobile families. When considering 'representativeness', however, it must be remembered that this is a small sample drawn originally from a single community.

The ethological bias of the research in the first year of the children's lives dictated that the children should always be seen 'on their own ground'. Subsequent research has almost all been done by home visits, partly for practical reasons and partly because of the advantages this offered for the research. For example, structured testing of some of the more reticent four year olds would have been extremely difficult in a less familiar context. Three visits were usually made at the four year old stage. The first was to the mother, the child usually being absent. The second and third visits were devoted to doing things with the child, and to observing the mother and child doing things together. The role-taking problems described in this chapter made up the second session, which was usually of about $1\frac{1}{2}$ hours duration.

Pilot studies and small-scale reliability studies were conducted with children attending a number of Cambridge infant and nursery schools, and the cooperation of the Local Education Authority and the head teachers involved is gratefully acknowledged. The main aim of this preliminary work was to establish which of a wide range of tasks discriminated well amongst four year olds, and then to discover the most suitable materials and administration procedures. The tasks were designed primarily for the establishment of meaningful individual differences in role-taking abilities amongst four-year olds. The question of the abilities of the group of four year olds as a whole was a secondary one, although of course the tasks threw some light on this. Margaret Craib, and Pamela Wirth helped with the testing involved in the subsidiary studies and Pamela Wirth also helped with testing in the main sample. Otherwise all testing was conducted by the present author, who will be designated as the observer ('O') in what follows. The child will be designated as 'C' where abbreviation is necessary. The children have been given pseudo-nyms which are sex-appropriate and used consistently throughout.

The tasks will be described in this chapter in an order chosen for clarity of exposition – a note of the actual order of administration will be found at the end of the chapter. For all of the tasks basic recording took the form of written notes made by the observer during the session on precoded blanks. This was supplemented in every case by audio tape recording which made available additional information including the children's utterances during the tasks. The children appeared not to be in the least disturbed by the tape recorder, which was fairly unobtrusive.

Perceptual role-taking problems

Most of the studies conducted by Flavell (1968) and colleagues were conducted with older children (see chapter 2), but he included a number of small-scale studies with 3–6 year olds. He employed mainly visual role-taking tasks, in which the child had to predict or take account of another's visual experiences under conditions in which these varied from his own. On the basis of these studies, Flavell suggests three closely-related 'acquisitions' of the preschool period. The child comes to know:

(a) how to infer whether a given stimulus is or is not visible to an observer, at least in simple situations;

(b) that when an object is interposed between himself and the observer, the observer will not see what he sees but will see the opposite side of the object;

(c) that when he and the observer sit opposite one another at a table and look at, say, a picture which lies flat on that table, then if he himself sees it the right way up the observer will see it upside down, and vice versa.

These three kinds of inference provide a useful way of classifying some of the tasks used in the present study. The first two tasks, for example, relate directly to the third point, and are, therefore, termed 'orientation' problems.

The first orientation problem

The first task was an extended and rather more carefully controlled version of one used by Flavell (1968, pp. 163–4), in which he found that about half of the mainly middle class three year olds tested and almost all of the five year olds could recognise that 'up the right way for me is upside-down for you.'

When testing in the children's own homes, the material ciricumstances inevitably varied somewhat from case to case. Usually a low table was available and the observer and the child sat on the floor. Occasionally a kitchen or dining table had to be used, with the participants sitting on chairs. This was only done if the child could see and reach the materials easily from his sitting position; in the few cases where this was not possible the game was played on the floor. These conditions applied similarly to most of the other tasks described in this chapter.

The object selected for the first orientation problem was a simplified two-dimensional human figure. A boy figure was used for boys, a girl figure for girls. To begin with O and C sat together on the same side of the table while the figure, lying flat on the table, was placed in a 'neutral' sideways position. O then turned the figure to a position such that both he and the child could see it the right way up and said e.g.: 'Look at this boy – he's up the right way isn't he? Standing up the right way.' O then rotated the figure through $180°$ and said: 'See, now he's upside-down, standing on his head, isn't he?' Returning the figure to the neutral position (this being done between all trials), O asked the child first to 'Put him so that we can see him the right way up, standing up the right way' and then to 'Put him so that we can see him upside down, standing on his head.' Of the sixty children, three were unable or unwilling to follow these instructions, all of the others were able to do this satisfactorily. The observer then stood up and went round to the other side of the table, drawing the child's attention to this by saying: 'Now if I go round *here...*', and then he asked the child to 'Put the boy so he's the right way up for me, so that *I* can see him up the right way.' The next instruction was to put the figure so that the child himself could see it up the right way, and then finally the child was instructed to put it so that *O* could see it upside down. Regardless of the child's placement of the figure, *O* always asked after each, e.g.: 'Can I see him up the right way? Are you sure?' These queries did force the child to consider, and sometimes to reconsider, his placements, but the child was never corrected explicitly. Figure 1 shows a child engaged in the task.

The sequence of 'trials' may be summarised as follows:

(*a*) Right way up for both *O* and *C*.

(*b*) Upside-down for both *O* and *C*.

(*c*) Right way up for *O*.

(*d*) Right way up for *C*.

(*e*) Upside-down for *O*.

The categories used for scoring children's performances are to some extent *post hoc*, adjusted to give a reasonable spread of scores since we

Figure 1. The first orientation problem

are primarily interested in individual differences. However, they attempt to retain the intended dimension of measurement, which one might call sensitivity to perspectives:

1. Placements correct ('decentred') on all trials, with no sign of confusion in responding. Some children made the underlying relationships verbally explicit, for example, Rhoda, on trial *e* (upside-down for *O*), placed the figure correctly and remarked that it was 'Standing up for me'.

2. Virtually correct, but with some confusion or need for nonspecific prompting. This category was used when the child hesitated doubtfully, so that the instruction had to be repeated before correct placement, or where an incipient error was spontaneously corrected before *O*'s standard query.

3. Correct except for one definitely incorrect ('egocentric') placement. In some cases there was an error on trial *c* (the first 'orientation-to-other' trial encountered) after which the child seemed to fully grasp the relationships involved. In other cases the final trial (upside-down for *O*) was failed after 'right way up for *O*' had been done correctly.

4. Predominantly 'egocentric' but with some sign of differentiation. This included a number of children who, although their initial placements were incorrect on both orientation-to-other trials, hesitated and changed their placements after *O*'s standard query. Some changed it and then changed it back again, seeming to know that it was wrong but not knowing how it should be.

5. Incorrect (egocentric) placements on all trials involving orientation-to-other. These were usually clear-cut performances, the figure being oriented in relation to the child himself on all trials, regardless of instructions and subsequent queries. This category does include some cases where errors were made on trials requiring orientation to *self*, but as will be seen the frequency of such errors was small. These were typically children who became inattentive after the first few trials, for instance Richard, who announced firmly that he had 'Run out of puff!'

To check the reliability of these categories a small group of nursery school children not involved in the project was tested and then retested a week later. Ten children aged between 3 years 11 months and 4 years 1 month were involved. A Spearman rank correlation coefficient was calculated between test and retest: $r_s = +0.85$ ($p < 0.01$). This indicated a fair degree of stability in individual differences on this task. There was in fact no overall improvement in performance on retesting.

In the main sample fifty-seven children gave scorable responses, the distribution across the range of scoring categories being given in table 3.1. The further analysis of these scores, including correlations with scores on other tasks and with other characteristics of the children, will be left to the following chapter (which will also be the case with the other tasks to be described in this chapter). Two points remain to be treated here. The first is the question of how far errors on this task can be construed as egocentric, as opposed to reflecting only confusion, misunderstanding or random responding. To examine this the number of errors made on trials requiring orientation-to-other may be compared with the number made on trials requiring orientation-to-self. This is done in table 3.2, where errors are further divided into inversions and others. Errors were scored as inversions when the figure was placed in a position 180° from the correct position. The category 'other errors' refers to less clear-cut responses where change of placement confused the picture, and to cases where the figure was placed in any orientation other than towards *O* or *C*.

While it is true that the child was given two opportunities to err on the orientation-to-other trials and only one on orientation-to-self, it is clear that this is not enough to account for the discrepancy in numbers of errors shown in table 3.2. The vast majority of errors involve orientation-to-other, and almost all of these errors are inversions.

A final question concerns whether these errors arise from the child's incomprehension of the perspective differences involved or from his lack of attention or sensitivity to this aspect of the task. The author's impression was that had he felt free to prompt the children explicitly and repeatedly, most of them could have been brought to a high level of

Table 3.1. *Scores on the first orientation problem*

Scoring	1	2	3	4	5
Number of cases	12	6	11	12	16

Table 3.2. *Pattern of errors on the first orientation problem*

Required orientation	Inversion errors	Other errors
To other	55	5
To self	4	2

competence on this task. This leaves open the question of what significance can be attached to the very considerable individual differences in performance observed on this task under relatively standard conditions: this issue will be taken up in later chapters.

The second orientation problem

This task was originally designed to pursue the question of the role-appropriateness of gifts chosen for others – again a measure suggested by Flavell (1968). A subsidiary question concerned the orientation of an object with respect to another person in a situation where the requirement was implicit rather than explicit. This initially subsidiary aspect of the problem actually turned out to be the more productive one.

Preliminary work with gift giving problems showed that it was difficult to get the children to justify their choices – if asked for reasons for choices they tended simply to say 'because' and leave it at that. This meant that one had to rely on the choices themselves in many cases, and often the decision as to whether a particular choice was appropriate or otherwise seemed highly arbitrary, depending upon stereotypes having little relation to the child himself or to his perceptions of the observer.

A game was devised which involved the observer and the child each having a set of cards and alternating the roles of giver and receiver. The alternation of roles was initially introduced simply because the children seemed to respond much better to tasks involving such alternation. *O* and *C* sat opposite one another and each had a line of cards in front of him, flat on the table. Each of the cards bore a single picture. The child's cards showed a doll, a scooter, a pipe and a hat. *O*'s cards showed an umbrella, a book, a toy train and a rocking horse. *O* asked *C* to name all the objects as the cards were laid down and then introduced the task by saying: 'Now let's pretend it's Christmas and we're going to give each other some presents. I'm going to give you (pause) an umbrella' (taking the umbrella picture and placing it in the child's line of cards) 'Now what are you going to give me for Christmas?' The child picked a card and placed it in *O*'s line. After the child's first 'gift' *O* repeated the procedure by giving the child a picture of a book. The child then made a further gift to *O* and so on to the extent of four exchanges. The situation is illustrated in figure 2.

The choice of the umbrella as *O*'s first gift reflected its ambiguity. It could plausibly be adult or child-appropriate (it was a red umbrella) and, more importantly, it did not have a definite 'right way up'. Although of course its appearance was dependent upon its orientation, neither orientation was clearly incorrect. When *O* took the umbrella card from his line he rotated it while putting it into *C*'s line, so that its orientation with respect to the child was the same as its orientation had been with respect to himself. The focus of interest in this task came to be in whether the child, in making his gifts to *O*, rotated his card in this way, so as to respect *O*'s perspective. Since all the cards were visible to both parties, the orientation of the other cards in *O*'s line provided a cue for the child, at least at first.

Four scoring categories were used in respect of the orientation of the cards given to *O* by the child:

1. All correct (the only allowable exception being a degree of confusion about the orientation of the pipe, which proved somewhat ambiguous). These children behaved as if the rotation of the pictures into the other's perspective was an obvious and 'natural' response.

2. Predominantly correct; an incorrect placement without spontaneous correction on not more than one occasion. Quite often cards were placed in *O*'s row and then rotated by the child. Sometimes incorrect

Figure 2. The second orientation problem

placements were corrected much later, at the end of the task, but this was not counted as 'spontaneous correction' for the purpose of this category.

3. Predominantly incorrect ('egocentric') but with definite indications of differentiation of perspectives, e.g. correct orientation of one card, or unprompted correction of card orientation at the end of the task. There were no cases where two cards were correctly oriented and two incorrectly.

4. All incorrect ('egocentric') with no indications of differentiation of perspectives. These children's performances typically had the same assuredness and naturalness as that of the children in Category 1. They seemed to see no problem in the fact that, at the end, all of O's cards as well as their own were 'their way up'.

Using these categories a small-scale test–retest reliability study was conducted with the same children used for this purpose in task 1. The Spearman rank correlation between performances one week apart was in fact the same as that for task 1, i.e. $r_s = +0.85$ ($p < 0.01$). Thus there seemed to be some stability in relative competence on this task.

In the main sample 57 children produced scorable responses. One was missed because the session was unavoidably curtailed and two were resolutely uncooperative! The overall results in terms of the numbers of subjects in each category are given in table 3.3.

It is interesting that, although scoring categories are not directly comparable, performance on this task did not seem to be markedly poorer than on the first orientation problem, despite the lack of explicit instruction to respect orientation. However, the fixed order of presentation of tasks prevents any very meaningful comparison from being made.

If errors of orientation reflected merely random placements we would expect a fairly high frequency of occasions where the picture was placed 'sideways' with respect to both O and C. In order to examine this, errors were divided into those where the card was placed sideways and those where it was placed the right way up for the child himself (i.e. 'egocentrically'). The resulting figures are given in table 3.4.

Table 3.3. *Scores on the second orientation problem*

Category	1	2	3	4
Number of cases	10	10	18	19

Clearly errors are not to be accounted for in terms of random placements of the cards. In fact many of the sideways placements involved the pipe, which was somewhat ambiguous as regards orientation, being put sideways by otherwise competent children.

With all the difficulties attached to the term 'appropriate', the appropriateness or otherwise of the children's gifts' assumed a secondary place. However, it was clear from some of the children's remarks that they were concerned about this. For example Cheryl's first gift was a hat: 'I'll give you a hat – you can wear it then' and Richard remarked that 'Men do have pipes'. Of the child's cards, we may regard the doll and the scooter as appropriate gifts for children but not for adults, and the hat and the pipe as appropriate for an adult male but not for children (the hat being definitely a man's hat). The particular cards chosen were only recorded for the first half of the sample. In this subsample, if we examine the first card selected for O by the child we find very slightly more inappropriate than appropriate choices. However, if we subdivide the children into those who are predominantly correct in orientation (categories 1 and 2) and those who are not (categories 3 and 4) we do find a relationship with the appropriateness of their first 'gift' to O. The children who are predominantly correct on orientation are significantly more likely to choose an appropriate gift ($\chi^2 = 3.94$, $p < 0.05$). This does lend some support to the idea that both orientation and gift-giving do reflect the same 'egocentrism'. However, it was not easy to devise a usable scoring system for appropriateness of gifts. For instance some children felt free to return cards given by O while others did not, which made the pattern confusing particularly with the later gifts. Therefore, the appropriateness or otherwise of choices on this task will not be considered further.

Two interposition problems
These tasks have to do with the second of Flavell's 'acquisitions' mentioned earlier: the realisation that when an object is interposed between the child himself and an observer, then the observer will not see

Table 3.4. *Distribution of errors on the second orientation problem*

Total errors	'Egocentric'	'Sideways'
141	122	19

what the child sees but will see whatever view is presented by the opposite side of the object. Flavell made a number of attempts to tap this realisation in his small study with preschool children (1968, pp. 166–72). The present procedures were developed with these in mind, although in their eventual form they show few resemblances to Flavell's tasks. The first problem requires the child to take the perspective of another person (the observer) with whom he is interacting. The second is similar except that the perspective which the child is required to adopt is that of a doll. The tasks will be referred to as Interposition (*O*) and Interposition (Doll).

Interposition (O): This task, developed like the others through pilot testing with nursery school children, involved a regular tetrahedon constructed of strong cardboard with pictures pasted on to three of its faces. When standing on the table it was in effect a three sided pyramid, about six inches high, bearing pictures of a teddy bear, a rocking-horse and a scooter. The advantage of the pyramidical shape was that, with *O* and *C* sitting opposite one another and looking slightly down on the object,

Figure 3. The first interposition task

then if *O* was looking directly at one of its faces the child could see the other two faces but could not see the face which *O* was looking at without actually getting up. Knowing the three pictures, the child could work out what *O* was looking at by a simple process of exclusion.

The procedure adopted was as follows: *O* and *C* sat opposite one another with a table between them. *O* placed the pyramid on the table and, turning it, got *C* to identify the three pictures one at a time and then to repeat the names of the three objects depicted. *O* then said: 'You hide your eyes while I turn this round till I'm looking at one of the pictures, O.K.?...open your eyes...what picture am I looking at do you think?' If necessary the question was repeated, but if the child did not eventually give a correct answer he was shown and told the answer. If the child did give the correct answer he was asked 'How do you know?'. Figure 3 shows the situation.

Roles were then exchanged, *O* covering his eyes while the child selected a face of the pyramid to look at. *O* guessed correctly and then the cycle was repeated so that the child guessed what the observer could see at least three times. All but one of the sixty children produced scorable performances. Scoring categories were as follows:

1. Children who were able to say which picture *O* was looking at without hesitation on each of the three trials. Often they explained the basis of their answer, e.g. Michelle said on the first trial: 'the teddy bear, because the scooter and the rocking horse is here'. The ready adoption of the other role on the trials when *O* was guessing was a condition of the child's inclusion in this category – a note on this aspect of the task follows later.

2. The second category covered children who failed to give a correct answer straight away on the first trial. They needed to have the question repeated, and often got up to look over the top of the pyramid. In many cases their difficulty was probably just forgetfulness, but it was not always possible to distinguish this from hesitancy with a different source. All of these children responded correctly and confidently on subsequent trials.

Table 3.5. *Scores on Interposition* (O)

Category	1	2	3	4
Number of cases	23	12	12	12

3. These were children who failed to give a correct answer on two of the three trials, or who on at least one occasion gave a wrong answer, suggesting that *O* was looking at one of the pictures which he was not looking at.

4. This lowest category of performance included all cases where more than one wrong answer was given, together with children who gave no right answers without prompting and did not seem to have 'got the idea' of the task even at the third trial.

The distribution of the fifty-nine cases between these categories is given in table 3.5. The figures reflect a fairly high general level of competence on this task. Relatively few of the children were able to explain the basis of their choices. Perhaps the most adequate answer was from Richard, who said that *O* was looking at the scooter because: 'We ain't got a bike [scooter] here, we got a teddy bear and a horse'. Difficulties of various kinds were encountered by the children in managing the alternate role, where *O* had to guess what *they* could see. For instance, both Brian and William told *O* what picture they were looking at before he had a chance to guess, and on another occasion Brian turned it round to show *O* as soon as he opened his eyes. Such observations suggest that children may find the situation in which they have to guess something that *O* knows more manageable than the situation in which *O* guesses something that they know. This point will be developed in relation to subsequent tasks.

Interposition (Doll): In this task the same three sided pyramid was used, together with a free-standing doll of appropriate height. The child was already familiar with the pictures on the pyramid as this task always followed directly upon the previous one. The doll was shown to the child and he was asked to name it. The child's name for the doll was used subsequently, but for the purposes of this account we shall call her Jenny. Figure 4 shows the general situation, while figure 5 shows a plan view with the various positions of the doll indicated by the numbers 1–5.

The doll was placed in poisition 1, facing the pyramid and the child was asked: 'What can Jenny see? What do you think Jenny can see?' The doll was then moved to positions 2, 3, 4 and 5 and the same question asked at each. Trials 1 and 2 may be termed single-face and trials 3, 4 and 5 double-face since on these the doll can 'see' two faces of the pyramid. On the double-face trials prompting was given where necessary. For example, if the child gave one of the two pictures visible to the doll, *O* asked: 'Can she see anything else, do you thing?' If the child said: 'Don't know' he was encouraged with 'Yes you do, what can she see?' If, as sometimes happened, the child said that the doll could see nothing, *O* replied 'Yes she can, what can she see?' This was the limit of the prompting given, and the need for prompting was taken into account in the scoring categories, which were as follows:

1. Correct answers on all trials without the need for prompting.
2. Answers on trials 1 and 2 given correctly. Correct on at least one of the double-face trials without prompting.

Figure 4. The second interposition task

Figure 5. The five positions of the doll in the second interposition task

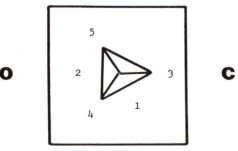

3. Answers on trials 1 and 2 given correctly but prompting needed on all double-face trials before a fully correct answer was obtained.
4. Failure to satisfy conditions for category 3 either through an error on one of the single-face trials (1 or 2) or because a full answer was not elicited even by prompting on one or more of the double-face trials.

Test–retest reliability estimates have not been made for the interposition tasks since the degree of within session learning (in the widest sense) made this impracticable. The distribution of scores for the 58 children tested is given in table 3.6.

As far as the single-face trials are concerned there is no indication that the children had more difficulty in taking the perspective of a doll than they had had taking the perspective of a real person in the previous task. We must acknowledge the possibility of order effects, however. The two tasks described in the following section also involve the use of dolls.

The large number of cases in category 3 reflects the considerable difficulty experienced by many of the children with the double-face trials (3, 4 and 5). As an illustration Richard, on trial 3, began by saying he could see 'nothing', and then said: 'there's that', pointing to the corner itself. Prompting from *O* elicited the answer: 'She can see the horse or the teddy bear', adding that she had got two eyes, as if to say that she could look at a different picture with each eye!

In this and subsequent tasks the naming of the doll by the child sometimes produced interesting results. Names frequently seemed to be attached to particular people; for instance Charles considered Katie as a name for the doll but rejected it because 'that's a baby's name'. It transpired that there was a baby called Katie across the road. The children often acted as if the doll must *have* a name which may or may not be known. When Shirley was asked 'What shall we call this doll?' she replied 'Don't know – I don't know her, do you?' When pressed to give her a name she asked 'Is she called Goldilocks?' *O* replied 'Goldilocks, that's a nice name' and Shirley exclaimed in a surprised tone '*Is* she called Goldilocks, oh, that's good!' This nominal realism, as Piaget called it (see Ch. 1) is just one of many phenomena shown in these tasks which may be interpreted in terms of a shift from absolute to relative perspectives.

Table 3.6. *Scores on Interposition (Doll)*

Category	1	2	3	4
Number of cases	5	18	28	7

Two hiding games

The first of Flavell's three kinds of perceptual inference, outlined earlier in this chapter (p. 35), concerns whether or not a particular object is visible to another person. The two tasks described in this section involve this type of inference. 'Hide and seek' games seem to provide an obvious approach, and anecdotes abound concerning the peculiar ways in which young children behave while playing such games. Indeed it is surprising that, apart from Hughes (1975), very little attention seems to have been given to such games by those interested in role-taking.

The use of dolls has obvious practical advantages, and also allows examination of how well the child can hold certain roles separate from one another (Hiding, *A*) and of how well he can coordinate roles (Hiding, *B*). The first task involves one doll being hidden from another amongst a group of 'obstacles' arranged for the purpose, while the second involves one doll being hidden from two others.

Hiding (A): Four obstacles were used to form the array in which one of the dolls had to hide. The obstacles were two dimensional representations of a house, a wall, a car and a tree and were constructed of painted board with blocks at the base so that they would stand firmly. Two wooden dolls about five inches tall were used, these being introduced to the child and named by him before the task commenced. The house and the wall

Figure 6. Positions of 'seeker' doll and obstacles in the first hiding game

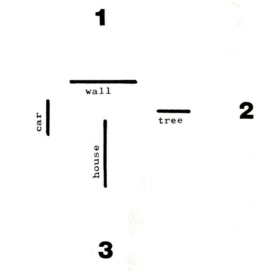

provided very good cover for a doll but the car and the tree did not, unless the doll was placed lying down behind the car or sideways (so that its arms did not stick out) behind the tree. The obstacles were disposed as in figure 6. Over four trials the 'seeker' doll began from each of the positions 1, 2, 3 and 4 in turn. Figure 7 shows the game, which was played on the floor as it required a fairly large space.

Giving the dolls the standard names of Jenny and Liz for the purpose of this account, instructions were as follows: 'First of all, Jenny's going to hide her eyes – she's going to stand over here (position 1, facing away from the obstacles) and she's not looking. Now, where can we put Liz where Jenny won't be able to find her? You find her a good hiding place'. When the child had done so, O turned the first doll round to face the array and asked: 'Can she see Liz?' The child typically answered 'No' and O then asked him to 'Take her to find Liz'. If the child did not do so, O demonstrated, but this was never necessary beyond the first trial. The task continued: 'Now *this* time Liz is going to hide her eyes and she's going to stand over *here* (position 2). Find a good hiding place for Jenny where Liz won't be able to find her.'

Figure 7. The first hiding game

For the purposes of scoring, mistakes were divided into two categories: minor and major errors. Minor errors included careless placements (e.g. leaving an arm or foot protruding), placements behind the car or the tree which did not use the limited cover effectively, and placements which were termed 'blind'. These were such that the 'hidden' doll was not visible to the 'seeker' doll from her initial position only because it was masked by some object approximately equidistant between the two. As soon as the 'seeker' doll began to move from her initial position these 'blind' positions were liable to come into full view. Major errors were such that the doll supposedly hidden was in fact openly and immediately visible to the 'seeker' doll as soon as the latter turned around to begin the search. The scoring categories adopted to discriminate levels of performance on the task were as follows:

1. No errors on any of the four trials.
2. A single minor error, otherwise all correct.
3. Two minor errors, otherwise all correct.
4. Three minor errors *or* a single major error.
5. More than one major error *or* errors of some kind on all trials.

Only two children failed to complete the task. The distribution of scores for the remaining 58 cases is given in table 3.7. Major errors usually involved the doll being hidden close to one of the obstacles but not behind it with respect to the 'seeker' doll. Marilyn always hid the doll so that she herself could not see it, but this was unusual. Almost all the children's performances included instances in which the doll was successfully hidden from the other doll while being visible to the child himself. Some of the major errors involved the doll being 'hidden' right out in the open, and in these cases the doll was always turned round so that it was looking away from the 'seeker'. Several children did something similar to this when hiding the doll behind the car: they realised that the doll's head was showing, but instead of laying the doll down they simply turned it around so that it was facing the other way. This seemed to reflect a confusion between *not being able to see* and *not being seen*.

Several mothers commented on parallel instances in playing hide and

Table 3.7. *Scores on Hiding (A)*

Category	1	2	3	4	5
Number of cases	6	17	11	17	7

seek with their children. For example Michael's mother said that when playing hide and seek he sometimes went away and hid his face: 'He thinks when he goes like this (covering eyes) he can't be seen.' Another mother commented on her children playing hide and seek in the garden: 'They hide behind a bush, but they don't think that half their bodies are showing... they're hidden if their faces are out of view but you can see all their legs and their jumpers and everything.' The reverse confusion was suggested by a remark of Kenneth's, who, when placing the 'seeker' doll at a point indicated by O before each of the trials, said to O: 'Don't look at her', as if the doll *not looking* (she was not to look while the other doll was being hidden) involved *not being looked at*.

Many of the children carried on a running commentary as they were deciding on a hiding place. For example. Cheryl: 'shall I hide her there?... then she won't see her... I think I'll hide her there (behind the car)... I think she will see her there (moved to a new place) she won't see her there.' Some of the children made an elaborate game of the searching ('she's going to look at the wall now...' etc.) often with a great deal of excitement. But much more frequently the children took the 'seeker' doll straight to the other's hiding place as if there were no uncertainty about the whereabouts of the other doll.

A number of children used the same 'hiding place' on all four trials, despite the inevitable lack of concealment on some of them. After Wilfred had placed the doll by the wall four times his mother remarked 'What an imagination you've got!' Anthony's mother illustrated a similar phenomenon in 'real' hide and seek games by asking him: 'Where do you usually hide when you hide from me?' Anthony: 'Under the settee' Mother: 'And if you're upstairs?' Anthony: 'Under the bed'.

These observations all reflect the richness of the situation as an approach to role-taking, and suggest that the role taking involved is not limited to inferring visual perspectives but pertains also to the motives and expectations of the participants.

Hiding (*B*): This task was similar to the previous one, but required a more complex coordination of perspectives. The same two dolls were used together with a third. The two obstacles used were each constructed from three painted boards and are shown in figure 8. Figure 9 shows a plan view with the various positions of the dolls indicated.

The child named the third doll, usually identifying it as male, so here we shall call him Nick. Presentation was as follows: 'Now in this game Nick is going to hide from *both* the girls. Jenny's going to stand here (at

A₁) and she's not looking. Liz is going to stand here (at A_2) and she's not looking. Now where can Nick hide where *neither* of them will be able to see him – where they won't be able to see him at all?' When the child had chosen a place, O asked 'Will that be a good hiding place?' This query sometimes led to a change of hiding place. Then O and C each turned one of the seeker dolls around and took it on a more or less elaborate search, culminating in one or both of them 'finding' Nick.

On successive trials dolls were placed at A_1 and A_2, B_1 and B_2, C_1 and C_2, D_1 and D_2 (see figure 9). The roles of the dolls were changed from trial to trial where the children suggested it. The configurations of dolls and obstacles permitted only one acceptable hiding place on each trial. The following scoring categories were used:

1. All four concealments correct and achieved directly, without even spontaneously corrected errors.
2. All four concealments eventually correct, but including one or more instances of erroneous placement spontaneously corrected by the child, or of the child moving around the array to 'line up' the perspectives of the dolls before placement.

Figure 8. The second hiding game

3. An erroneous placement left uncorrected, or corrected only after O's query: 'will that be a good hiding place?'
4. Such an error on more than one occasion.

All but two of the children completed the task and the distribution of scores is given in table 3.8. The results indicate that 41 of the 58 children eventually reached a correct solution by themselves on three of the four occasions. Even allowing for the relatively simplified situation this is perhaps a surprisingly high level of performance. There were, nonetheless, considerable individual differences.

The spontaneous correction of errors (category 2) sometimes involved systematic trial and error, but more often a single careless placement was quickly followed by the realisation of error ('Here...no *she'll* see him!') Moving around to take the viewpoint of the dolls (category 2) was allowed but only happened in one or two instances.

Sometimes little nuances of behaviour showed how well the children had grasped the situation. Shirley, for instance, took great pains to tidy the doll's hair so that it wouldn't stick out and make her easier to find. Several children engaged O in hiding games when the task was over, and these games were often interesting. For instance Stan peeped through his hands when O was hiding something in the room. When allowed to look he made no pretence of looking in other places first, but went straight to where he had seen O put it, denying nonetheless that he had seen this. Richard also highlighted the difficulty young children have in concealing their own knowledge of something: he noisily went over to a tuffet and hid the doll behind it, calling to O (who was hiding his eyes): 'I aren't ready yet – I'm going to hide it just here, don't you do cheat or I won't

Figure 9. Positions of 'seeker' dolls and obstacles in the second hiding game

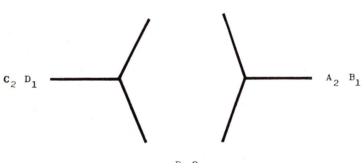

play then.' Then as soon as *O* began looking around, Richard got very excited and said 'I hid it, it's over there', pointing to where it was hidden!

A few of the children created their own imaginary games. Denise, for example, drew upon the fact that one of the obstacles was painted with trees and the other with houses. She also introduced a much smaller doll of her own. Here is a small part of her 'running commentary' on her game:

A littly tiny one hide there and they all both going to look for the little baby one: 'find! find! find!' Then (they find) the baby 'Oh poor'. And him come and pick the baby one up and carry baby to mummy. 'look, baby coming' and take his coat off 'cos it's a very good sunny day at home now – him in the house lying down in the shade. Sue have a sleep with jumper on, get so warm no-one can't find her; me put her there, there's a good hiding place for her...(to *O*:) you take her and look for a giant, a boy giant, in the forest. Her in the house, little one in the house. They (girl and boy giant) not can't see a baby. Mummy looks and sees them and (she says): 'Oh, a giant, not can't come in, the little beeby very quiet' and she tells the giant off 'No you can't come in there, 'cos me kill you' and then him fell dead.

In this type of imaginary play the child is both creating and taking roles, assimilating the dolls, the game and the whole situation into an elaborate fantasy.

Penny-hiding: a social guessing game

The use of social guessing games to examine aspects of role-taking was discussed in chapter 2 (pp. 21–2). It is arguable that such open-ended techniques bring us closer to 'real life' role-taking situations than do the techniques discussed so far, in which there are clear right and wrong answers. In social guessing games we are dealing with a chain of inferences on the basis of which the child has to make a 'best guess' about what to do in a given situation.

In De Vries' (1970) study the hiding of a penny in one of two hands formed the basis of the problem. She suggested on the basis of this and previous studies that age changes in behaviour in this situation reflect a

Table 3.8. *Scores on Hiding (B)*

Category	1	2	3	4
Number of cases	13	9	19	17

shift from acting without taking the 'game role' of the other into account to acting in terms of an anticipation of the other's behaviour. Both De Vries (1970) and Berner (1971) simply asked the child to 'guess which hand the penny is in' as the observer's hands were repeatedly hidden behind her back, and then invited the child to hide the penny for the observer to guess. The essentials of the second part of the task are properly hiding the penny, taking care not to let *O* see the penny until after he has tried to find it, and changing the hand in which the penny is concealed between some trials, but not every time. Berner identified failing responses as, for example, always hiding the penny predictably in the same hand, or letting *O* see where the penny was hidden, since these behaviours indicated that the child was not putting himself in *O*'s place and planning his behaviour accordingly.

The procedure adopted in the present study was as follows. The observer showed the child a penny and said that they were now going to play a guessing game: 'I'm going to hide the penny in one of my hands (doing so behind his back) and you've got to guess which hand it's in (bringing his hands out, fisted, in front of him). Which hand do you think

Figure 10. Penny-hiding: first stage

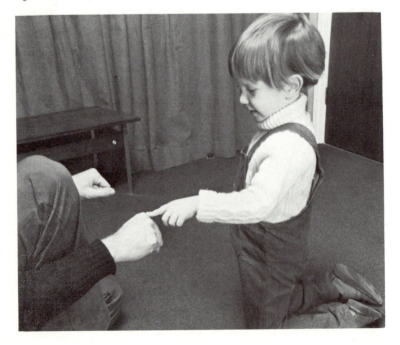

the penny is in?' (see figure 10). The observer hid the penny seven times in all; for the first three trials he 'cheated' by using two pennies so that the child was right every time. Then for the next three trials he had a penny in neither hand, so that the child failed every time. Two pennies were used on the last trial. This ensured that children all had the same experience of success and failure. None of the children detected that *O* was cheating in this way. *O* then said: 'Now it's your turn to hide the penny – hide it just like I did and I'll try to guess which hand it's hidden in' (see figure 11). Six trials were given for scoring purposes, although many of the children were keen to continue the game apparently indefinitely. *O* attempted to guess wrongly except where it would be obvious to both parties that he was doing so and excepting also the last of the six trials. In general, as will be seen from the results, it was not difficult to know which hand the penny was actually in!

The principal scoring system used, known as the concealment score, was made up of three items scoring 1 or 0 and three items scoring 2, 1 or 0, making a possible range of 0–9 points. The scoring criteria are set out below:

Figure 11. Penny-hiding: second stage

A. Needs prompting on more than one trial to get the basic 'mechanics' of the hiding role established (1 point).

B. Only one hand presented, or the two hands held conspicuously differently (first occasion 1 point, more than once 2 points).

C. The empty hand actually open while visible to O (first occasion 1 point, more than once 2 points).

D. Penny actually visible to O for any reason (first occasion 1 point, more than once 2 points).

E. Giving away the location of the penny by looking at it, fiddling with it, etc. (1 point).

F. Telling O which hand the penny is in, or is going to be in (1 point).

Overall scores for 57 children are given in table 3.9. The remaining three children refused the task. The frequency of occurrence of each of the scoring indicators is given in table 3.10.

The common failings of the children in adopting the 'hiding' role can be seen from the prevalence of the various component items of the concealment score. Most of the children seemed to be able to deal with the notion that they could open their hands and swop the penny about while it was behind their back but not while it was in front of them. The majority, however, were not able regularly to bring out their fisted hands and hold them symmetrically. Thus there was not usually any difficulty for O in guessing which hand contained the penny, quite apart from the give-away predictability of sequence which was characteristic of so many of the children.

This issue of the sequence of the child's guesses or his concealment

Table 3.9. *Concealment scores in the penny-hiding game*

Total general score	0	1	2	3	4	5	6	7	8	9
Number of cases	2	9	13	14	8	6	3	2	0	0

Table 3.10. *Distribution across scoring indicators in the penny-hiding game*

Criterion	A	B		C		D		E	F
Points	1	1	2	1	2	1	2	1	1
No. of cases:	15	20	23	15	16	13	2	17	9

was approached through a subsidiary scoring system, which may be termed the *sequence* score. This was made up of a guessing score and a hiding score, each being a measure of the regularity of the child's behaviour over trials. Two types of regular sequence were involved. In the first (called a straight sequence) the child always guessed that the penny was in (or hid the penny in) the *same* hand. In the second (called an alternate sequence) the child systematically alternated between left and right hand in guessing or in hiding the penny. Sequences were classified as nearly regular if a regular sequence was broken on only one occasion. Giving two points for a fully regular sequence and one point for a nearly regular sequence, each child could be given a sequence score in the range 0–4. The distribution of scores obtained is given in table 3.11. The overall frequencies of regular and nearly regular sequences in hiding and guessing are given in table 3.12. Data are presented only for the first half of the sample – the reasons for discontinuation of the sequence scoring at this stage in the study will be discussed in the next chapter.

These results show that regular sequences were extremely prevalent both in guessing and in hiding. There is no evidence to support De Vries' (1970) finding that sequences in guessing were significantly more regular than sequences in hiding. On guessing trials, breaks in the sequencing almost always followed a failure to find the penny on the previous trial. There was often a pronounced hesitation before the choice which broke the sequence. Breaks in the regular sequence of hiding seemed to have a variety of causes. In some cases the penny was dropped by the child,

Table 3.11. *The sequence score on penny-hiding*

Total sequence score	0	1	2	3	4
No. of cases	0	3	7	16	3

Table 3.12. *Frequencies of various kinds of sequences in penny-hiding*

Guessing	Straight	Regular	0
		Nearly regular	7
	Alternate	Regular	9
		Nearly regular	10
Hiding	Straight	Regular	3
		Nearly regular	6
	Alternate	Regular	12
		Nearly regular	6

or he changed the penny from one hand to another after O had guessed (i.e. he cheated). That most of the children were treating the task competitively and enjoying O being wrong was clear from their comments. For example Wilfred remarked gleefully to his mother: 'He keeps missin' don't he?' Rhoda actually instructed O before one trial: 'You think it's in the same one' and then hid the penny in the 'other' hand so that O would be wrong. Elaine went so far as to leave the penny behind her on the last trial, so that neither hand contained the penny, but she was unable to resist opening both hands before O had had a chance to guess and said, with much laughter: 'That tricked you!'

Alternating sequences were much more common than straight sequences overall. De Vries (1970) proposed that the straight strategy should be regarded as more primitive than the alternating strategy. This suggests that in the present study, children who adopt an alternating sequence should tend to have a lower concealment score (i.e. should perform better) than those who adopt a straight sequence. In fact the mean concealment scores for these two groups are 3.0 and 2.9 respectively, this result obviously failing to support the contention that either one type of sequence is more 'primitive' than the other.

Was the penny hidden more frequently in one hand than in the other? Overall there was no significant difference, but if all the children who alternated regularly are excluded there is a marginally significant excess of right hand concealments ($\chi^2 = 2.81$, $p < 0.1$). This suggests that, other things being equal, there may be a slight preference for hiding the penny in the dominant hand. As to guessing, the total number of guesses of O's right hand and his left hand were exactly equal, so that there was clearly no preference. A bias towards selecting O's dominant hand might have seemed to suggest very sophisticated role-taking indeed!

Faces: sensitivity to others' emotions

The tasks described so far have largely omitted the affective side of role-taking. This was discussed in chapter 2 (pp. 22–3) with particular reference to the studies by Borke (1971, 1973), in which she presented children between 3 and 8 years of age with a series of short stories. They were asked to indicate how the child in each story felt by selecting a 'happy', 'sad', 'afraid' or 'angry' face to complete the picture accompanying each story. A version of this task was included in the present study both because it complements some of the biases of the other tasks, and because the relationship of individual children's abilities on this task to their abilities on other types of role-taking measure is of considerable interest.

A set of ten stories was composed and four inkwash pictures of boys' faces and four of girls' faces were drawn for the author by David Birtwhistle. Each set of four included a happy, a sad, a frightened and an angry face all mounted on thin plywood cut-outs (see figure 12). A blank faced cut-out figure of appropriate sex was used, boy faces being used by the boys, girl faces by the girls.

The child named the figure; in this account we shall use the name David. The observer remarked on David not having a face and showed the child the four faces, putting each onto the figure in turn and asking: 'How's David feeling now?' Any reasonable synonym for the emotional expression was accepted but if the child was doubtful or (as very occasionally happened) actually wrong in his interpretation, O prompted or corrected as necessary.

The faces were laid out by the side of the cut-out figure, to the child's right. The order of the four faces was altered between stories, the ordering being arbitrary except that the most appropriate choice occurred twice in each of the four possible positions (ignoring the first story, which was primarily introductory). The stories were as follows, prompting and correction being used in relation to the first of the stories only:

Figure 12. Materials used in the 'faces' task

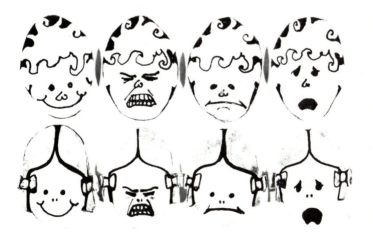

Story 1. 'Show me how David would feel if he had a lovely new toy as a present. Would he feel cross, sad, scared or would he be happy? (pointing to each face in turn). Yes, he'd be happy, wouldn't he? So you pick the happy face and put it on David.' If the child did not say happy, or point to the happy face, *O* supplied the answer.

Story 2. 'One night David was asleep and he dreamed that a great big *tiger* was chasing him. How do you think David felt when he dreamed that the tiger was chasing him? Which face would he have?'

Story 3. 'David had a pet rabbit which he loved very dearly but one day he went out to feed it and he found that his rabbit had died. Show me how David felt when he found that his pet rabbit had died.'

Story 4. 'How would David feel if he was playing with a ball and you just went and snatched it away from him and wouldn't give it back. Which face would he have when you took his ball away?'

Story 5. 'David likes ice cream. Show me how he would look if the ice cream van came round and his mummy bought him an ice cream.'

Story 6. 'If David was playing on his tricycle and you pushed him off it on purpose, how would he feel? What face must we put on?'

Story 7. 'Sometimes David wants somebody to play with but can't find anybody to play with him at all. How does he feel then?'

Story 8. 'If you pretended to be a ghost and ran after David in the dark, what would he be?'

Story 9. 'And if you asked him to come to your birthday party, what would he be then?'

Figure 13 shows a child responding to one of the stories. Note that in many of the stories the child is discouraged from simply casting himself in David's role by being himself portrayed in the stories as acting towards David in a complementary role. It will be clear from a consideration of the stories that it is not possible on every occasion to distinguish one correct from three equally incorrect answers. This was dealt with by distinguishing three categories of choice, the middle category covering choices which, while not being those intended as appropriate by *O*, are still relatively plausible. Table 3.13 illustrates this rather *ad hoc* procedure, which was made necessary by the inevitable slight ambiguities of interpretation of the stories and by the less than complete predictability of emotional responses.

It was clear from results of pilot work that the *happy* face was very much easier for the children to deal with than the other faces. This is reflected in the scoring system adopted. The index of competence with the remaining faces was devised to take account of the possibility of response bias, and also to make it easier to incorporate the scores of those few children who for one reason or another did not complete the full nine stories. The child's use of any one of these faces was counted as *inappropriate* if, taking all the occasions upon which the child selected that face, the choice fell into the -1 category more frequently than into the $+1$ category (see Table 3.13). Choices in the zero category were thus effectively ignored. The full scoring system used is set out below:

1. Fully correct ($+1$ choices on all nine stories).
2. Not more than one of *sad*, *scared* and *cross* used inappropriately as defined above.
3. More than one of *sad*, *scared* and *cross* used inappropriately as defined above.
4. Child uses the *happy* face improperly; either by not always selecting it where appropriate, or by selecting it where inappropriate.
5. Child could not get idea of matching faces to stories at all. Very confused responding persists despite prompting.

Figure 13. The 'faces' task

Fifty-eight of the children were scored according to these categories; one was missed through an oversight and one was too shy to participate. A number of children became 'fed up' with the task before the full nine stories had been given. Where it was not possible to hold their attention, scoring was based on the results of fewer than nine (though never fewer than five) choices. Fortunately, the fifth scoring category was not needed very often. The distribution of subjects between these five categories is given in table 3.14.

The children's verbal responses for the most part reflected their choices. They were useful on a few occasions when they clarified a misinterpretation of the story by the child. Marilyn, for example, explained that the child in story 8 was happy 'because she had a goat to play with'! Where such explanations made sense of a choice which would otherwise have been incorrect it was not scored against them, but such instances were rare. Most of the stories seemed to be understood as they were intended. The pattern of errors for story 7, however, seemed to reflect a partial exception to this; *cross* was never chosen, but quite a number of children chose the *scared* face. Perhaps they were responding to 'not being able to find anybody' as frightening, and taking this element of the story out of context.

Table 3.13. *Categorisations of choices in the 'faces' task*

Story	Intended choice	Relatively plausible alternatives	Implausible choices
I	Happy	—	Sad, scared, cross
2	Scared	—	Sad, happy, cross
3	Sad	—	Happy, scared, cross
4	Cross	Sad, scared	Happy
5	Happy	—	Sad, scared, cross
6	Cross	Sad, scared	Happy
7	Sad	Cross	Scared, happy
8	Scared	Cross	Sad, happy
9	Happy	—	Sad, scared, cross
Scored	+1	0	−1

Table 3.14. *Scores on the 'faces' task*

Categories	I	2	3	4	5
No. of cases	3	22	18	12	3

Since all the children in the first three categories use *happy* appropriately throughout, it is clear that the happy face was used most adeptly, which is in agreement with the findings of Borke (1971). Of the remainder, the *sad* face was used more frequently than the *cross*, and the *cross* face more frequently than the *scared*, but all three were used with roughly equal accuracy.

This completes the account of the role-taking tasks used in the study. Together they made up one testing session of about one and a half hours duration. The order of administration did not quite coincide with the order in which the tasks have been described, but was as follows: Orientation (1), Faces, Orientation (2), Interposition (*O*), Interposition (Doll), Penny-hiding, Hiding (*A*), Hiding (*B*). Since the order was the same for all cases, possible 'order effects' upon performance cannot be examined, although they might in themselves make an interesting study. For the present our primary interest is in the wide range of individual differences found in a group of four year old children doing the same tasks in the same sequence. The intercorrelations of scores of individual children across the range of tasks will be the first concern of the following chapter.

4

Role-taking: a composite measure

In the first part of this chapter the statistical intercorrelations of scores derived from the role-taking problems and games will be presented and interpreted. In the second part of the chapter the validity of a composite role-taking score will be examined through some preliminary investigations of its relationship with other data available on the four year olds.

Correlations

Scores are available from eight tasks described in chapter 3, all of them supposedly tapping aspects of role-taking. The convergent validity of role-taking as a construct can be investigated by examining the intercorrelations of the eight scores. Table 4.1 shows the resulting correlation matrix, the number of cases (N) varying slightly but being never less than 50. The coefficients are uniformly positive with an average value of about $+0.4$. Twenty-four of the 28 coefficients are statistically significant at the $p < 0.05$ level.†

Before considering these correlations any further, we shall digress to consider the results for a ninth measure: the sequence score derived from the penny-hiding game.

† Product–moment correlation has been used, as it extends readily into more complex forms of analysis. The scores employed do not meet all the assumptions associated with this technique, but the deviations (e.g. differences in distribution form) should on the whole be conservative in their effects (Nunnally, 1967). However, the significance levels should be treated with caution. As a check, Kendall's τ was used to reanalyse data from the first half of the sample. τ values ranged from $+0.22$ to $+0.72$ with an average value of about $+0.5$, all but one being statistically significant.

Note that $p < 0.05$ will be regarded as a satisfactory level of statistical significance throughout, and will be denoted by an asterisk in the tables. All comparisons are 'two tailed' unless specifically stated.

The sequence score

Correlations between the sequence score and the eight other measures are shown in table 4.2. Sequence data were collected only for the first half of the sample, so that *N* varies between 27 and 29. This measure is clearly the 'odd man out' since its correlations with all the other scores are negative, and half of them significantly so. The derivation of the sequence score was discussed in the previous chapter in relation to the study by De Vries (1970) who used irregularity of sequence in hiding and guessing as one of her indices of the child's role-taking ability. Certainly with older children one would not expect to find the highly predictable sequences evidenced in the present study, but it is hazardous to equate an irregular pattern of guesses or concealments with a 'shifting strategy'. An irregular pattern might reflect no strategy at all. It may be that for very young children the successive guesses or concealments are in effect independent of one another, with the child not construing them as forming a coherent sequence at all. Some anecdotal observations mentioned in the previous chapter support this view, which would also throw some light on our failure to replicate one of De Vries' findings. She found that sequences

Table 4.1. *Intercorrelations of role-taking scores* (*$p < 0.05$, 2 tailed*)

	1	2	3	4	5	6	7	8
1 (Orientation, 1)		+0.52*	+0.42*	+0.34*	+0.24	+0.35*	+0.37*	+0.45*
2 (Orientation, 2)			+0.38*	+0.32*	+0.37*	+0.45*	+0.48*	+0.46*
3 (Interposition, O)				+0.40*	+0.33*	+0.12	+0.45*	+0.56*
4 (Interposition, Doll)					+0.19	+0.24	+0.54*	+0.33*
5 (Hiding, A)						+0.59*	+0.43*	+0.46*
6 (Hiding, B)							+0.40*	+0.32*
7 (Penny-hiding)								+0.51*
8 (Faces)								

Table 4.2. *Correlations of the sequence score with the other eight scores (numerical designations of scores as in table 4.1)*

	1	2	3	4	5	6	7	8
Sequence score	−0.06	−0.43*	−0.01	−0.30*	−0.30*	−0.32*	−0.18	−0.10

in guessing were significantly more regular than sequences in hiding, suggesting that deceptive hiding is easier than guessing and may precede it developmentally. It is worth noting, however, that the only study in which De Vries used subjects under five years old (1970, Study I) failed to support her other findings on this point. If we suppose that our present results relate to a developmentally earlier stage at which regularity of sequence represents an advance towards eventual deceptiveness, then we can predict from De Vries' own position that sequences in hiding would be more regular than sequences in guessing, which would be more in line with our findings (Ch. 3, p. 60). So the suggestion being made is that irregularity of sequence may not reflect intentional deceptiveness at all; on the contrary those children who follow a very predictable sequence may be nearer to following a 'shifting' sequence than those who follow no sequence at all. Since the correlational results so clearly indicate that the sequence score is aberrant, and since a plausible explanation may be put forward to account for the more adept role-takers tending to use more regular sequences, the sequence score was dropped, and will be omitted from further considerations.

Interpretation of the correlations
A point of interest in relation to table 4.1 is that the 'penny hiding' and 'faces' scores relate well to one another and to the other scores, all of which reflect performance on visual perspective-taking problems. However, bearing in mind the strictures of Masters and Wellman (1974), only limited significance should be attached to particular values within the correlation matrix. What is clearly shown in table 4.1 is that all the eight scores being considered intercorrelate positively, and for the most part substantially. Given that the tasks were all chosen to tap aspects of social role-taking, the most obvious interpretation of these positive inter-relationships is that they reflect generalisable individual differences in role-taking ability or sensitivity. It seems unlikely that the correlations simply reflect shared method variance, in the sense discussed by Shantz (1975), since the measures are quite dissimilar in content and in the types of responses required. We can examine this point in conjunction with another possibility: that the scores relate to one another only because they all relate strongly to something more general, the obvious candidate being the 'general cognitive capacity' of the children. Taking IQ as an index of such capacity, the question becomes how far are the intercorrelations of the role-taking measures secondary to a common correlation with IQ?

Intelligence

In the third of the home visits carried out when the children were four, the Stanford–Binet Intelligence Scale was administered, using the Wright method of abbreviation (Terman and Merrill, 1961, p. 83) which cut down administration time to about one hour. The author was fully trained in the use of this test. The IQ's obtained ranged from 95–145, with a median of 122. This is somewhat higher than was expected, given the social backgrounds of the children, and might reflect the selection biases mentioned in the previous chapter. Nearly all of the children were attending a nursery school or playgroup, and it may be that this relatively new state of affairs is associated with improved test performance in this age range. In any case, our present concern is only with individual differences in IQ and their relationship to the role-taking measures. Table 4.3 shows the relevant correlation coefficients (N between 55 and 57).

All correlations are positive and some are substantial. Partial correlations were calculated in order to examine the relationships of the role-taking measures to one another with the effects of IQ held constant. These are shown in table 4.4.

Table 4.3. *Correlations between IQ and the eight role-taking scores*

	1	2	3	4	5	6	7	8
IQ	+0.58*	+0.40*	+0.47*	+0.27	+0.30*	+0.23	+0.43*	+0.61*

Table 4.4. *Matrix of partial correlations*

		2	3	4	5	6	7	8
1		+0.38*	+0.20	+0.24*	+0.09	+0.27*	+0.16	+0.15
	2		+0.23*	+0.24*	+0.28*	+0.40*	+0.37*	+0.30*
		3		+0.32*	+0.22*	+0.01	+0.31*	+0.39*
			4		+0.12	+0.19	+0.49*	+0.22*
				5		+0.56*	+0.35*	+0.37*
					6		+0.34*	+0.23*
						7		+0.35*

All the partial correlations are positive, and 21 of the 28 coefficients reach statistical significance on the one tailed test judged appropriate here. These results, then, demonstrate a considerable degree of intercorrelation between these measures quite apart from their relationship to IQ.

This to some extent covers the 'shared methods' point raised earlier, since an individual IQ test at this age is made up of items having many of the same game-like characteristics as the role-taking measures. Insofar as the role-taking scores do relate to IQ, two aspects of this relationship are worth considering. First, all the role-taking measures have a puzzle solving aspect, and for this reason one would not expect them to be independent of IQ. Since the IQs are based upon a well established test whose high reliability is related to its long administration time, there should be a high ceiling to correlations with any other measure. Second, and of more interest perhaps, is the idea that the IQ test might have a role-taking aspect. An individually administered IQ test involves a protracted social interaction in which it is critical that the child readily understands what the tester intends by his questions. To an important extent the child's problem is to identify the implicit character of the social situation, to 'see what kind of game is being played'. Consider for example the year five Stanford–Binet question 'What is a ball?' All the children in the present sample clearly knew in some sense what a ball was but few could answer this question in the test. They seemed not to know what sort of answer was required. In framing an answer the child has in effect to take the perspective of one who does not know what a ball is, even though he may recognise that the examiner himself does know. These considerations may be particularly salient for the preschool child, for whom the formal testing situation is a very strange one.

Principal components analysis

In order to investigate the interrelationships of the eight role-taking measures more thoroughly, principal components analysis of the eight role-taking scores was carried out, the technique being similar to that used in the studies by Rubin (1973) and Hollos and Cowan (1973) discussed in chapter 2. In the few cases where one of the eight values was missing, the overall mean score on that measure was inserted. Where more than one of the eight values was missing, the case was dropped from the analysis. This left a sample of 26 boys and 30 girls.

Table 4.5 presents the resulting components, eigenvalues and proportions of the total variance accounted for. The most striking thing shown by this table is the very large first principal component, which by itself accounts for approximately half of the total variance. Applying the usual criterion that only eigenvalues equal to or greater than 1.00 should be considered significant (Van de Geer, 1971), we shall give further consideration only to the first and the second components derived from this analysis.

Table 4.6 shows eigenvectors for each of the eight measures on the first two orthogonal components. The 'loadings' of all eight measures on the first component have the same sign and are very uniform. On the second the loadings range from markedly positive to markedly negative. One way of presenting these figures is to lay them out spatially along coordinates representing the two components under consideration, as in figure 14. This shows up a tendency for certain of the measures to sort into pairs on the second component. The two hiding measures (5 and 6) have high positive loadings while the two interposition measures (3 and 4) have high negative loadings. The orientation measures (1 and 2) show low loadings, as do the remaining tasks (penny-hiding and faces).† These pair-wise groupings presumably reflect similarities within (and contrasts between) the pairs of measures, either at the level of the materials and formats employed, or at the level of the particular kinds of spatial inference required (Ch. 3, p. 35). This interpretation would enable us to regard the second, and possibly subsequent, components as tapping task-specific variance, so that we might look to the uniform loadings on the large first component to provide a relatively 'pure' measure of that

Table 4.5. *Principal components analysis (eigenvalues)*

Components	1	2	3	4	5	6	7	8
Eigenvalues	3.77	1.11	0.79	0.78	0.49	0.42	0.36	0.30
Cumulative proportions of total variance	0.47	0.61	0.71	0.81	0.87	0.92	0.96	1.00

Table 4.6. *Principal components analysis (eigenvectors)*

Role-taking scores	1	2	3	4	5	6	7	8
1st component	+0.67	+0.73	+0.67	+0.60	+0.65	+0.62	+0.76	+0.77
2nd component	−0.16	+0.08	−0.46	−0.38	+0.53	+0.65	−0.12	−0.09

† On the third component the two orientation measures have substantial negative loadings, while all others are positive.

general aspect of role-taking which the tasks share: the awareness of the need to adapt to another's viewpoint. However, although the internal evidence supports such an interpretation, it cannot be confidently made without using external criteria, and to try to predict the external concomitants of these several components in order to differentiate their significance would seem premature in such a little known area.

A composite role-taking score based on all eight measures was needed in order to investigate hypotheses, considered in chapter 2, concerning which children should be adept role-takers and which not. Rather than relying on our interpretation of the first principal component and using it as the basis for such a composite score, the more straightforward procedure of simply summing the eight scores was adopted.† The resulting scores (which we shall presumptively call role-taking scores in

Figure 14. Loadings of the eight role-taking measures on the first two principal components

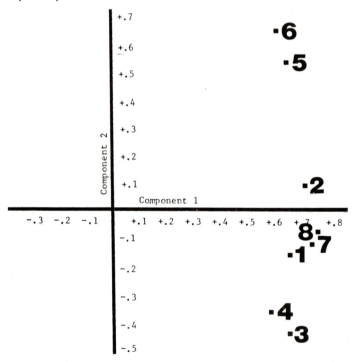

† In practice the outcome was not much different either way, due to the large size of the first component. The use of a simple sum score was judged to be adequate since the means and distributions of the eight scores were broadly similar and the achievement of exactly equal weightings was not crucial.

what follows) for 56 children showed an approximately normal distribution with a mean of 22, a range of 9–37 and a standard deviation of 6.5. These scores form the basis for the further investigations of role-taking in following chapters.

In the remainder of the present chapter some basic information about the families, together with data from interviews with the mothers, will be employed in an examination of some of the more obvious predictions about role-taking. The overall role-taking score correlates significantly (+0.6) with IQ, so as a general rule the relationships established with role-taking will also be examined in terms of IQ to get some idea of their specificity.

The maternal interview

An extended interview, taking one to two hours, was conducted with the mother of each of the children in the sample. This was done in a separate session from the observation and testing of the child. The range of topics covered was dictated partly by the central interests of the present study and partly by more general considerations concerning the longitudinal study of the children's development. John and Elizabeth Newson's *Four Years Old in an Urban Community* (1968) was an important influence both on the questions asked and, more significantly perhaps, on the way in which they were asked.

The questions were 'open ended' and the whole interview was tape recorded for later transcription. The questions were paraphrased and 'probe questions' added where appropriate. Most of the questions related to fairly specific situations, with examples both given in the questions and asked for in the response. Nonetheless the mothers' attitudes and expectations were clearly reflected in their answers to questions about their children's behaviour. The questions did not usually provide a clear cut scale for possible answers, and the mothers' frames of reference (in terms of their knowledge of other four year olds) were often rather limited. The question of mothers' attitudes etc. is taken up at appropriate points in the discussion of the interview findings.

The sequence of questioning was not completely rigid, as often mothers would effectively cover some of the later questions in their answers to early ones. In general the mothers appeared not only very willing to talk about their children, but to actually enjoy having a good listener! The interview seemed to be successful in getting a good deal of information about the mothers' childrearing attitudes and practices without giving them the feeling of being 'judged'. Transcription was not verbatim except for examples and for sections relating to discipline and control (see Ch. 5). A precoded form was used to achieve a primary categorisation of answers. This form was developed on the basis of 'pilot' interviews.

Play

If we ask what aspects of the child's everyday behaviour might be expected to show relationships to his role-taking abilities then one of the first to come to mind is role-playing, or 'role-enacting' in Sarbin's sense (Sarbin, 1954; see Ch. 1). Mead (1934) discussed role-playing as a corrolary of role-taking, and, as noted in the first chapter, he placed much emphasis on play in his account of role-taking development. In this section we shall consider the data available from the maternal interview relating to various aspects of play.

The main question concerning role play was 'Does he play games where he pretends to be someone, like a teacher or a shopkeeper or a daddy...?' Supplementary questions concerned the child's favourite role, whether he alternated between complementary roles, whether he only played this sort of game with other children. Children were divided into those described as playing such games very frequently both with other children and by themselves, and those who played such games rarely, usually only under the influence of an older sibling. A difficulty encountered was that while the boys distributed fairly evenly between these groups, the girls were almost all described as prolific role-players. This sex difference was significant statistically ($\chi^2 = 8.0$, $p < 0.01$). Amongst the boys, those manifesting a lot of role-play were significantly better scorers on the role-taking measure ($p < 0.05$)† but this relationship was swamped out when treating both sexes together.

If the association between role-taking and role-playing provides limited support for Mead's contentions, what about his idea concerning the more advanced stage of the 'game'? This is characterised for Mead (see Ch. 1) in terms of a coordinated structure of rules and goals, within which the players' roles are represented. Arguing more generally from Piaget's position, the egocentric child would not be expected to accommodate to the constraints of pre-existing rules, which would evince instead a distorting assimilation on the part of the child. Piaget (1932) discussed the development of the child's participation in rule games and interpreted this development in terms of egocentricity.

† Independent sample *t* tests are used in such comparisons throughout this account.

In the light of this, mothers were asked about rule games in the interview: 'Does he ever play any games with *rules*, like "remember-remember" or ludo or anything like that?' The mothers were thus prompted to think in terms of card games or board games. Here there was no pronounced sex difference. Twenty of the children were described as not playing any rule games, or only very simple ones like 'I spy' occasionally and not very well. Twenty-seven mothers answered the question affirmatively and gave examples of the games played. There was a considerable variation in the range of games played and in the child's enthusiasm for them, but all these 27 children were described as being able to play largely by the rules and accept at least occasional defeats! The remaining cases were uncategorisable for one reason or another. The children who participated in rule games were, as predicted, significantly better scorers on the role-taking measure ($p < 0.02$). This provides some validation for the latter measure especially since there was no significant association between answers to the question and the child's IQ.

Similar relationships emerged with another aspect of the child's play which mothers were asked about: symbolic play. For Piaget, symbolic play is a sign of childish egocentrism, while for Mead fantasy play in general is a part of the developmental process towards reflective thinking and role-taking (see Chs. 1 and 2). In the interview, mothers were asked: 'When he's by himself, does he often use things pretending that they're something else – like using chairs for a train or buttons for soldiers?' In 15 cases this was answered in the negative, or with reference only to a few occasions on which the child had participated in, say, a game of 'buses' on the sofa with an older sibling or other child. In 36 cases symbolic play was described as common (more common with large 'props' than with small ones). Comparing these groups, again there was no significant relationship with IQ but there was a significant relationship with the role-taking measure ($p < 0.05$). The children who were reported to engage in a good deal of symbolic play were those more competent at role-taking. This suggests that symbolic play should not be regarded as an *indicator* of egocentrism, as Piaget has implied, but rather as an indicator of the process whereby egocentrism is transcended.

These subtler aspects of imaginary play may not be very reliably reported; some mothers seemed to notice everything and some almost nothing. Also attitudes clearly varied: Richard's mother said 'He's usually pretty good' meaning that he uses things for what they are rather than for what he can pretend they are. Some mothers saw symbolic play as something children only have to do if they haven't got the real thing (e.g. Denise's mother: 'She doesn't have to substitute') while others clearly valued and enjoyed their children's imaginary play in all its forms, and went into great detail in their accounts.

The importance of solitary role-taking in play was discussed in chapter 2, and a direct question on solitary play was included in the interview: 'Does X seem to enjoy playing by himself a lot, or will he only play by himself when there's absolutely no-one else to play with?' Seventeen children were described as having a strong preference for social play and being unwilling (or unable) to play by themselves at all. The remaining 37 cases were described as playing by themselves when necessary, and occasionally even for preference. The former group were marked poorer on the role-taking measure than were the latter group ($p < 0.001$), but in this case the same relationship was shown with IQ, though at a lower significance level ($p < 0.05$).

Social experience with peers
Although the capacity for solitary play has been shown to relate positively to role-taking abilities, there is good reason to suppose that social contacts with other children may be important for the development of role-taking. Piaget's emphasis upon the importance of the peer group was noted in chapter 2, where a variety of opinions on this issue were discussed.

Rather surprisingly, none of the children in the sample were 'only' children at age four. Sixteen were first born children and the remainder second born. A comparison of first borns and second borns in relation to role-taking showed a significant difference, second borns scoring better on the role-taking measure ($p < 0.05$).† There was no birth-order difference in IQ scores.

Mothers were asked about the 'closeness' of the children to the sibling nearest in age, in terms of how well they played together and how much time they spent together. Those described as very close in these respects tended to be the better role-takers but this relationship did not reach statistical significance. Almost all the children had some experience of nursery schools or playgroups, but since this varied so much in terms of how long and how often they had been attending and also in sizes of groups and kinds of activities engaged in, it proved impossible to compare children in respect of such experience. The interview contained

† This finding indirectly conflicts with other evidence on role-taking and birth-order (see Shantz, 1975).

questions relating to the child's social contact with other children apart from siblings and apart from playgroups etc. The picture that emerges is of an intermediate group being better role-takers than those who have only very occasional contact (less than once a week) with other children, but also better than those having daily contact with a number of other children.

A similarly complex picture emerges using a quite different source of data. A modification of the 'Standard Day' interview technique (Douglas, Lawson, Cooper and Cooper, 1968) was used with a subsample consisting of the first twenty families. The mother was asked to recall exactly what the child had been doing during the immediately preceding 24 hours. While giving her account, which was tape recorded, she was prompted by the interviewer towards consideration of who the child was with and the degree of involvement between the child and those he was with. The fullness of the record was somewhat variable, but on the whole, once they got started, the mothers' recollections were sufficiently detailed. The recall interview was done twice, on separate occasions, with each mother. Each transcript was analysed twice; once to categorise it in terms of the amount of time spent in various levels of interaction with other children, and once to similarly categorise interaction with adults. The categories were taken from Ingleby and Lawson (1971). Of particular interest are the measures of time spent in 'concentrated' (exclusive) interaction either with adults or with other children. A high level of concentrated interaction with adults was significantly associated with good role-taking scores ($p < 0.05$). There was no significant relationship between amount of concentrated interaction with adults and the child's IQ, confirming the findings of Lawson and Ingleby (1974). As regards concentrated interaction with other children the picture is again complex, with those children who experienced an average amount of peer interaction being better at role-taking than those experiencing either much more or much less.

These findings, together with those from the main interview, seem to suggest that the amount of adult attention is much more directly related to role-taking than is the amount of interaction with other children. This tends to contradict Piaget's emphasis on peer relationships, being more consistent with the proposals of Flavell (1968) and Kohlberg (1969) discussed in chapter 2. However, no very strong relationships are indicated, lending support to the conclusion of Lawson and Ingleby (1974) that one will probably get further by examining the quality of the interactions involved than by pursuing measures of quantity. This line of approach will be taken up in the following chapter.

Further information from the general interview

A number of questions in the interview concerned the children's actual social behaviour. Mothers were asked how good their children were at sharing and cooperating with other children. Marked sex differences emerged in the answers. For instance exactly half of the boys were described as 'good sharers' whereas only one in eight of the girls were so described – this difference being significant statistically ($p < 0.01$). Similar sex differences were shown in answers to questions concerning aggressive behaviour and temper – for instance twice as many girls as boys were described as being aggressive towards other children. These sex differences, running counter to widely held expectations about boys and girls, almost certainly reflect the different expectations which mothers have for the two sexes in these matters. They may thus act as a reminder that we are dealing with the child *as seen by the mother* in this interview material.

There were no significant relationships between role-taking abilities and answers to any of these questions. This result suggests that if there is any relationship between social behaviour and role-taking, then it is not a simple and obvious one. A good deal more light will be thrown on this problem when data obtained at other points in the longitudinal study are examined in chapter 6.

Another interview question which turned out to be more revealing of mothers' attitudes than of their children's behaviour was: 'Does he sometimes tell you fanciful things, that you know are not true, just for the sake of telling them?' Apart from the cases where this was simply answered in the negative, twelve mothers took this question to relate to 'fibs', false denials and so on, of which they naturally disapproved. The remaining 25 mothers provided instances of 'fanciful' untruths of the sort intended by the question. This seemed to reflect the attitudes of mothers towards 'imagination' and it turned out rather strikingly that the twelve mothers who treated fanciful untruths as lies had children who were significantly poorer on the role-taking measure ($p < 0.02$). Even amongst those providing instances of 'fanciful' untruths there was a great variation in expressed attitudes. Some referred disparagingly to the child 'talking rubbish', while others spoke indulgently of fantasy, creativity, and 'romanticising'.

A number of questions in the interview concerned the 'clingingness' or dependence of the child. The questions dealt with how often the child sought the mother's attention when she was busy with something else, how often the mother had to 'start the child off' and give him periodic attention during play, how strongly the child tended to play in the vicinity of the mother rather than elsewhere, and how much initial difficulty there was when the child first went to playgroup or nursery school. A composite score based upon the answers to these four questions showed a significant correlation with both role-taking ($+0.3$, $p < 0.02$) and IQ ($+0.3$, $p < 0.02$) scores. The less dependent the child, the better his role-taking and IQ scores tend to be. Flavell (1968, p. 221) comments that he would be 'intrigued to find out whether children with high dependent and affiliative needs...are especially precocious in acquiring [role-taking] abilites'. Present findings suggest quite a different picture. The examination of relationships between four year old role-taking and earlier data available on these children in chapter 6 will help to clarify this issue.

Sex and social class differences
Some of the measures discussed above in relation to role-taking might also be expected to relate to social class indices, and some certainly show sex differences. If the present measure of role-taking abilities were to show a strong relationship to sex and/or social class, we might have to question how far this accounted for the significant relationships discussed in the previous sections.

The role-taking score did not show a significant sex difference, there being a slight but quite nonsignificant trend in favour of girls. Rather more surprisingly, perhaps, the role-taking score was not significantly associated with social class either. The occupational status of the father was classified according to the Registrar General's categories. Classes I, II and III (white collar) were grouped ($N = 27$) and compared with classes III (manual) and IV ($N = 29$). Although there was a tendency for higher status families to have children who were more adept at role-taking, this did not reach statistical significance.†

† A measure related to social class, but bearing more directly upon the child's world, is the educational status of the mother. Mothers were divided into those with some GCE 'O' or 'A' levels or equivalent ($N = 32$) and those with no formal educational qualifications ($N = 27$). This dichotomy was related to the role-taking measure, though only just at a significant level ($p = 0.05$).

A summary

In the first part of this chapter a statistical analysis of the scores derived from the eight 'role-taking' tasks was presented. The regular pattern of intercorrelations suggested the derivation of a unitary measure of 'role-taking ability' for the purpose of investigating some of its external correlates. In the second half of the chapter some of the more obviously predictable relationships were examined, using basic information about the families together with information from an extended interview with the mother.

The measure derived from the role-taking tasks was found to relate significantly to interview measures of playing rule games, symbolic play, liking for solitary play and, for boys, role-playing. The role-taking measure did not show significant sex or social class differences, but second born children did score significantly better than first borns. Information from the general interview and from the 'standard day' interview showed a significant positive relationship between role-taking and the amount of concentrated adult attention, but a more complex relationship to amount of interaction with other children. Amongst other points considered from the general interview were several questions relating to independence; good role-takers seeming to be relatively independent children.

These results confirm some of our expectations about the concomitants of role-taking, but they are for the most part very crude findings. The next chapter will attempt a more subtle characterisation of the mothers and their relationships with the children, in the hope of identifying some of the factors which are of importance in the development of sensitive role-taking.

5

The child and his mother

Towards the end of chapter 2 the suggestion was made that the patterns of interaction and communication in the child's family must provide an important setting for role-taking opportunities. In particular, the relevance of Bernstein's work was noted. Bernstein (1965, 1970, 1972) has analysed the relationship between the child's behaviour and cognitive development on the one hand and the structure of relationships within the family on the other. He points to the style and content of communications as providing the key to this relationship: 'According to this view, the form of the social relation...generates distinctive linguistic forms or codes and these codes essentially transmit the culture and so constrain behaviour' (1965, p. 149). Bernstein has characterised two kinds of communication codes, or styles of language, which he has termed 'restricted' and 'elaborated'. Restricted codes are stereotyped, limited and condensed, lacking specificity and precision. They arise where the form of the social relation is based upon closely shared identifications and common assumptions. In elaborated codes, communication is individualised and the message is specific to a particular situation, topic or person. It is more differentiated and more precise, and intentions are made more explicit. Elaborated codes are related to person-oriented interactions whereas restricted codes are related to status-oriented interactions (see Ch. 2, p. 29), although this is not a simple 'one to one' relationship, as later work (e.g. Cook-Gumperz, 1973) has shown. Hess and others in Chicago (Hess and Shipman, 1965; Hess, Shipman, Brophy and Bear, 1969) have developed these distinctions. They suggest that a status-oriented or 'positional' statement, for example, tends to offer or imply a set of regulations and rules for conduct and interaction, rather than basing conduct upon consideration of particular consequences. Elaborated and 'person-oriented' statements lend themselves more easily to styles of cognitive approach that involve reflection and reflective comparison. Hess and Shipman conclude that elaborated codes may lead to the child learning to 'role play with an element of personal flexibility' (1965, p. 873).

In this chapter we will pursue this sociolinguistic approach, using it particularly to examine what the mother says to, and about, her child. In the first part of the chapter the mother's speech to the child in an instructional situation will be analysed. In the second part of the chapter the 'positional/personal' dichotomy touched on here and in chapter 2 will be applied to interview data relating to the mothers' social control strategies.

Research on mothers' teaching strategies

Various studies of factors related to successful communication have demonstrated social class differences in the ability to label and encode the critical features of a situation (e.g. Baldwin, McFarlane and Garvey, 1971; Heider, 1971). Such studies, in the context of the recent interest in the processes which underlie 'cultural disadvantage', have focussed attention on characteristics of the parent's language in different socioeconomic status groups. Olim (1970) has reviewed this research.

Hess and colleagues approached this problem in a study involving urban negro mothers and their 4 year old children, who were divided into four social status groups. Variables studied included language styles, cognitive styles, problem solving behaviour, socialisation practices, control strategies and teaching behaviour in deliberate instructional situations. Differences between mothers in the various groups were found in all these measures, and maternal scores were systematically associated with child measures.

In summary, Hess and Shipman (1965) have described the behavioural deficit amongst the 'culturally deprived' in terms of a lack of *meaning*. Particular acts appear to be insufficiently related to preceding or subsequent acts, and are not sufficiently related to the motivations of the participants or to the goals of the task.

Brophy (1970) has concentrated on the situation in which the mothers were required to teach their own 4 year old children. The mother was first taught a simple task (block sorting along two dimensions) and was then observed while attempting to teach it to her child. In general,

Brophy's results suggested that the differences observed amongst the mothers were not so much differences between two or more specific teaching styles, but ranged along a continuum from the restricted, repetitive and reactive at one extreme to the elaborate, varied and proactive at the other. The most pronounced differences occurred in three areas. The first of these was the degree to which each mother attempted to motivate her child by presenting the task as an enjoyable experience, by encouraging his efforts and by praising his success. The second was the degree to which the mother provided an introduction to the task before launching into it, and the third, closely related, was the degree to which she gave specific pre-response instructions describing the cognitive operations required of the child. Many of the 'lower class' mothers tried to show the child what to do with a quick demonstration and then settled into a pattern of eliciting a response from the child and trying to teach him by corrective feedback.†

This kind of teaching situation was seen to have a number of advantages for the purposes of the present study, although our interest is not so much in social class or other group differences as in the relationship of individual differences amongst mothers to individual differences amongst the children, especially with respect to role-taking. Effective communication in teaching depends upon the mother being able to adopt the child's perspective. To teach the child a task she has to make a general adjustment to his being a four year old child, and to what she knows of his capabilities. More specifically, she has to adjust to his ignorance both of the aims of the task and of how to achieve them. Since the overall content to be communicated is similar for all mother–child pairs, we may use this situation to examine individual variation in the form of these adjustments.

The teaching task

A new task was designed, intended to be sufficiently difficult for the four year olds to need extensive help, but easy enough for their mothers to be able to grasp it with a minimum of verbal instruction. The task in its final form involved wooden blocks each 1 in. by 2 in. by 2 in., and each coloured on both ends. In Part I of the problem eight blocks were used. Half of these were coloured red at both ends, while the other half were

---

† Social class differences in maternal teaching strategies have been further documented by Bee, Van Egeren, Streissguth, Nyman and Leckie (1969), while Steward and Steward (1973) have studied ethnic differences in a similar fashion.

red one end and blue the other. The blocks were to be placed in a long box which had a flap coloured red for half its length and blue for the other half; the blocks had to be inserted so that the colour on the top of each block matched the colour on the flap opposite it. In order to achieve this, blocks which were red on both ends had to be placed in the box at the 'red' end, while blocks red on one end and blue on the other had to be placed, blue side up, at the 'blue' end. Part II of the problem was similar except that nine blocks were used, and the flap of the box showed red, *black* and blue sections. The red/red blocks and the red/blue blocks were as before (three of each), but now there were three blue/black blocks in addition, which had to be placed black side uppermost for the problem to be solved. Part II was simply intended as a more complex version of Part I, and was included both to enlarge on the information available on each dyad and to make it reasonably certain that all the children would meet with difficulties at some stage.

The teaching task was introduced at the beginning of the first of the sessions in which the observer was planning to work with the child, and the task was represented to the mother as a way in which she could 'break the ice' with the child before the observer took over. The mothers seemed to accept this and did not see their own performance as being the object of evaluation. Where possible the child was not in the room when the mother was being told about the task. In cases where this was not possible the child was distracted with a toy at this point. The blocks for Part I of the task were presented to the mother in their proper places in the box. Her attention was drawn to the required matching of colours between the top of the blocks and the flap, and then the blocks were lifted out by the observer and the 'other ends' were shown to her. She was told that the task involved taking all the blocks from the box, putting them into a cloth bag, shaking them up and then withdrawing them one by one and placing them correctly in the box. The verbal instructions were as standardised as possible, given the need to answer questions and to make sure the mother understood the task properly. In practice all the mothers grasped the essentials of the task readily. All the blocks were then replaced correctly and the mother was asked to 'Show that to X, see if you can teach him how to do it'.

When the child had completed the task to the mother's satisfaction, Part II of the task was presented. The child was asked to go out of the room while the observer showed this more elaborate version to the mother. The children regarded being sent outside until their mother called, 'Ready!' as being a part of the game. Both ends of the blocks were shown to the mother as before; no additional instructions were usually necessary. The task was carried out in exactly the same way as Part I.

The intention was that the child should be dependent upon the mother to provide a context of meaning within which he could understand the task. The tasks were unfamiliar to all subjects, but the materials and goals were easily specified and responses were clearly correct or incorrect. Preliminary piloting suggested that the difficulty level was such that the great majority of subjects would be able to complete the tasks eventually, but not without considerable guidance and help from their mothers.

Tape-recording provided the principal means of recording the session. This was supplemented by written notes made on precoded sheets by the observer at the time, the function of which was to note the order in which the blocks were taken from the cloth bag and whether each was placed correctly or incorrectly. This information was needed in order to interpret the transcript of the tape recording. Categories for analysis of the transcript reflect the aspects of teaching strategy which have been found interesting in previous studies, but have been considerably adapted. Each will be discussed in conjunction with the relevant section of the results.

Perhaps the best overall criterion for the task is the time elapsing from the beginning of instruction to the child's completion of the task. The overall average was about seven minutes. Since the time data were heavily skewed, they were transformed logarithmically for analysis. To examine some of the determinants of total time a two-way analysis of variance was done using sex of child and mothers' educational status (A- or O-levels vs none) as factors. The analysis showed no significant sex difference, but a significant main effect in the predictable direction for mothers' education ($p < 0.05$) and a significant interaction term ($p < 0.05$) which arose because the effect of mother's education was shown strongly with girl children but hardly at all with boys. Separate analyses showed the maternal education effect to be highly significant ($p < 0.01$) amongst the girls and completely absent amongst the boys.

The relevance of the mothers' education measure may be direct (being associated with their competence in the teaching role) or indirect, being merely a reflection of more general social class differences. To investigate this the above analysis was repeated, substituting the Registrar General's classification of the fathers' occupations (I + II + III (white collar) vs III (manual) + IV). The result was a quite nonsignificant effect of fathers' occupation on total time, and no sign of an interaction with the sex of the child.

Short total times are significantly, though not strongly, correlated with high role-taking scores amongst the boys ($p < 0.05$) but not significantly amongst the girls. However, it is perhaps more meaningful to separate the time the mother spent in instructing the child from the time the child spent actually doing the task. The term 'introduction' will be used to denote the period from the beginning of the mother's instruction of the child to the point at which she let him take the first block out of the bag to begin the task. The period from the end of the introduction to the end of the task will be designated 'completion'.

We might expect to find that where mothers spend a long time instructing their children, the children need less time to complete the task. A significant inverse relation between introduction time and completion time is indeed shown by the boys ($p < 0.02$) but is quite absent among the girls. The length of introduction is not itself associated with the mothers' educational status, which in the light of the findings for total time suggests that better educated mothers are needing less time overall, but are devoting a higher proportion of it to introduction: a proactive rather than reactive strategy.

Another individual measure obtained from the children may be brought in at this point. A version of Kagan's 'Matching Familiar Figures' test (Kagan, Rosman, Day, Albert and Phillips, 1964) was used as an index of 'reflective' vs 'impulsive' cognitive style. This test requires the child to select from amongst a set of slightly varying pictures the one which is identical to a given 'standard' picture. Following the arguments of Garner, Percy and Lawson (1971) the impulsivity measure was based only on response latencies preceding erroneous answers. The matching familiar figures test was administered on a separate session from the teaching task presently under discussion. This measure of impulsivity showed a significant relationship to the length of introduction amongst the boys, though again not amongst the girls. This is striking, since the length of orientation is dependent almost entirely upon the mother's behaviour, rather than upon the child's.

Better role-taking scores were associated with longer introduction time amongst boys, but nonsignificantly. It is predictable, therefore, that completion times should be substantially shorter for boys with good role taking-scores, and this was so ($p < 0.005$). At a lower level of significance shorter completion times were also associated with higher IQ ($p < 0.05$) and more 'reflective' cognitive style ($p < 0.05$) amongst boys.

The picture which seems to emerge is that the 'mother-measure' (mother's educational status) accounts for much of the variance in teaching times amongst the girls, while the 'child measures' (role-taking, impulsiveness, IQ) account for much of the variance amongst the boys.

A number of aspects of the transcripts were examined in an attempt to identify qualitative characteristics of the mother's teaching style. Hess and Shipman (1972) concluded that the more successful mothers tended to praise their children a good deal, as well as giving them more specific instructions. In the present study praise was often given for specific block placements as well as at the end of the task, and took such forms as 'Jolly good...that's super', 'You're doing very well aren't you?', or 'Clever old stick in't you?' About two thirds of the mothers used this kind of praise at some stage. There was no significant difference between those who used praise and those who did not in terms either of the mother's education or of the child's IQ. However there was a positive association between the use of such praise and the role-taking ability of the child, this being significant ($p < 0.05$) on a one tailed test.

In order to examine the question of specificity of instructions the transcripts were categorised in terms of whether the mothers made the goal of the task (the matching of block tops with the coloured flap) and the critical feature of the blocks (that they may have different colours on each end) verbally explicit to the child. Rather surprisingly, such explicitness in instruction did not show any relationship to the mother's educational status, the child's IQ, or the role-taking measure. Informal observation suggests that this lack of association may reflect the fact that some mothers tried to avoid making the task 'too easy' for their children.

There was a broad dichotomy in terms of the ways in which mothers dealt with the child making an error on the task. On the one hand the mother might point out the error immediately and get the child to correct it then and there (e.g. 'No, that's not right is it?' or 'No, you've got to have it so that the pink piece is at the top.'). On the other hand the mother might let the error go, perhaps with a 'warning' remark, and wait until the child came up against the consequential difficulties before starting to help him (e.g. 'Something's gone wrong somewhere, hasn't it?' or 'You'll have to look at the pink ones and see if you put them in right.'). Only corrections relating to the placement of a block the wrong way up were considered in this analysis, and cases where there was one or more instance of 'deferred' correction were compared with the cases (comprising about a third of the sample) where correction was always immediate. These groups were markedly different in terms of the child's role-taking abilities ($p < 0.01$), deferred error correction being associated with competent role-taking. A similar though less pronounced relationship existed with the child's IQ ($p < 0.05$).

Summarising these findings in relation to the role-taking measure, it seems that amongst the boys mothers of good role-takers gave as much or more initial introduction to the task as others, but the completion time was substantially shorter, as was overall time on the task. For both sexes such mothers praised their children more and they tended to allow the child to encounter the consequences of his own errors before attempting to help him correct them. While it was true that amongst girls the mother's educational level is predictive of total time (and completion time) on the task, it does not seem that this reflects a very general social class difference. The other measures discussed (praise, error corection etc.) do not show significant relationships to mother's educational level or to the Registrar General's classification of father's occupation. These findings, taken in conjunction with the non-significant relation of the role-taking measure and the occupational status index (see Ch. 4) suggest that the relationships established between role-taking and aspects of the mother's teaching strategy are not merely reflections of general social class differences. However, social class differences in maternal teaching styles have been demonstrated in other studies (e.g. Brophy, 1970) and it is acknowledged that the present sample may not be well suited to showing them. The conventional social class distinctions may not be as useful in a city like Cambridge as elsewhere. Where there is no strong industrial tradition and a predominance of 'service' occupations it may be that social segregation along occupational lines is less complete. The conditions for the establishment of a 'working class culture' may not be as well met in Cambridge as in, say, Nottingham (cf. Newson and Newson, 1968).

Social control and the mother–child relationship

In the introduction to this chapter and in chapter 2 Bernstein's work was discussed, particularly his characterisation of family relationships in terms of a personal-positional dimension. To recap from chapter 2, Bernstein (1970) has suggested that in a 'person-oriented' family the individual intentions, motives etc. of the family members are constantly realised verbally in their speech to one another, and the child's developing self (or self-awareness) is progressively differentiated as a consequence of this. In a 'positional' family, speech typically makes implicit or explicit reference to status requirements, and the child learns a more communal and less differentiated role. It seems likely that the distinctions which Bernstein is drawing here should relate closely to the development of the role-taking abilities of the child. Indeed it is hard to think of a more appropriate characterisation of those aspects of family interaction which could be expected to relate to the development of such role-taking.

Bernstein has suggested that these characteristics of family relationships may most directly influence the child through the means of social control employed in the family. Bernstein and Cook (1968) have developed a coding frame dealing with distinctions between various forms of social control (described in detail in Cook-Gumperz, 1973). A somewhat abbreviated form of this has been employed in this study. The primary source of data used is the maternal interview described in the previous chapter. The interview was designed to contain a range of questions touching on social control and disciplinary situations. Since an 'open-ended' interview technique was used, mothers usually elaborated on their answers to specific questions and provided a good deal of information how they handled certain situations and why they adopted one strategy rather than another. Those parts of the interview which touched upon these issues were transcribed verbatim from the tape recording.

The first and broadest level of analysis, taken from the Bernstein–Cook coding frame, deals with the mother's rationales, the reasons she gives to the interviewer for acting in a particular way. In the first place the mother's reasons may be related to herself or to the child. Consider for example: Esther's mother: 'She gets me in such a temper that...' as against Elaine's mother: 'If she's really ashamed of herself...'

Bernstein goes on to distinguish those rationales referring to mother or child in a personal fashion (as in both of the above examples) and those mentioning positional attributes. In practice very few statements were coded as positional (e.g. Stella's mother: 'Children have to learn that mother is busy too'). The scarcity of positional rationales could be related to the fact that the lowest social class groups (IV and V) were barely represented in this sample. Cook-Gumperz (1973) found a much higher level of use of positional rationales in the lowest of her social class categories than in the middle and higher groups.

What did emerge in the present study was a great variation in the frequency with which personal rationales for action were given, particularly in reference to the child. Such qualifying remarks typically 'get below the surface' of the child's behaviour and consider things from the point of view of the child's feelings, intentions and character. To give another example, Caitlin was said to get a smack 'if she's told someone she doesn't like them and she *means* it, that's what I don't like'.

Such a characterisation leads one to expect that the frequent use of such 'person-centered' rationales by the mother should be associated with good role-taking abilities on the part of the child, and this turned out to be the case ($p < 0.05$). Although the correlation coefficient is not very large ($+0.3$) the result is notable in the light of the absence of even a marginally significant relationship between the use of such 'person-centered' rationales and the child's IQ. The relationship between the child's role-taking abilities and the mother's use of personal rationales with respect to herself (e.g. Barney's mother: 'Depending on the mood I'm in...') was not statistically significant.

Actual control strategies used by the mother were examined in the light of the categories employed by Bernstein and Cook. The open-ended nature of the interview and the resulting variation in 'richness' of transcripts made it difficult to decide how best to approach the analysis. Rather than applying categories of control strategy 'across the board' it seemed more satisfactory to use particular questions in the interview as indices of particular kinds of control strategy. For each of the categories the question was selected which gave the highest frequency of responses falling into that category.

The first category is *avoidance* – involving attempts by the mother to avoid the problem being seen as a problem. The interview question which acts as the best 'indicator' of this tendency to avoid involvement where possible concerned the way in which mothers dealt with quarrels between their children. Rather over half of the mothers described themselves as adopting a 'low profile' in this situation, either doing nothing (e.g. 'Usually if I can stand it it wears itself out') or trying to placate the children and suggesting something else for them to do. Other mothers intervene in such a way as to assert their dominant role in the situation, which may involve punishment or removal of disputed possessions (e.g. 'I just go in there and take it away from both of them – lock everything up and say you can't have them out until you've learned to share them'). Comparison of these two groups showed a marked association with the child's role-taking abilities. 'Low profile' mothers tended to have children with relatively good role-taking ability ($p = 0.005$).

The second main category of social control is physical punishment. While this clearly overlaps with other questions, the interview did include one direct question on smacking. About two thirds of mothers rated their use of smacking as at most occasional – once every week or so for particularly serious things. The remainder said they smacked their children most days and for a wide variety of offences. Michael, for instance, was said to 'live on smacks'. These two groups are significantly differentiable in terms of the child's role-taking abilities ($p = 0.001$), frequent smacking being associated with poor role-taking. Some of the maternal attitudes which underly this relationship may perhaps be seen in the following quotation from Alice's mother, answering a different question:

> I explain why they shouldn't do it you know, but whether she's old enough to grasp what I'm trying to tell her or not I don't know. If I threaten to pull her hair hard that does more good. She's only just turned four so you can't really expect her to understand what I'm trying to get through.

The third main category of control strategy distinguished by Bernstein and Cook is *support*. Under this heading, three subcategories are identified: emotional support, concessions and bargaining. These cover the mother's use of positive rather than negative incentives.

The best question for eliciting instances of emotional support was the question concerning the mother's handling of the child's temper tantrums. Not all of the mothers gave categorisable replies, as such tantrums are by no means a universal phenomenon. Of the replies about a quarter were classified as instances of emotional support. Kenneth's mother provides an example: 'Feeling embarassed is often the cause... I'll have to really cuddle him and comfort him.' Since emotional support is of necessity personal rather than positional in the senses defined earlier, we might expect an association between such emotional support and good role-taking on the part of the child, and this is indeed the case ($p < 0.01$).

The question used to index concessions and bargaining was: 'What happens if you ask him to do something for you and he says that he can't because he is busy in the middle of a game or something?' This was clearly a familiar situation. For the purposes of analysis those answers were identified in which the mother stated that where things were not especially urgent she accepted the child's 'busyness' as a valid excuse, at least for a limited time. This was sometimes quite an explicit concession (e.g. 'Well, I don't bother her then, if she really thinks she's busy I let her get on with it') or more typically had an element of bargaining (e.g. 'If he says he's doing something I'll say "do it when you've finished" and he will'). The remaining mothers, classed as not respecting the validity of the child's 'busyness', gave answers such as Caitlin's mother: 'I usually say: "You'll do it now – I've told you to do it."' This division is again significantly related to the role-taking abilities of the children ($p < 0.02$), concessions and bargaining being associated with adept role-taking.

Caitlin's mother's 'I've told you to do it' brings out the way in which mothers in the 'no concessions' group see it as an issue of authority. The mother of the lowest scoring child on the role-taking measure (Brian) added: 'I don't like the way some people perhaps say "will you do this for me?" and then don't insist.' In contrast, mothers in the 'concessions' group frequently gave answers which were suggestive of a symmetry between mother and child. For example, the mother of the child scoring most highly on the role-taking measure (Michelle) recognised that she herself didn't like being interrupted: 'Yes, she'll perhaps not do it straight away, but then I'm like that. If I'm busy doing something I'll say well wait a minute – so it works both ways I suppose.' Warren's mother used the same symmetry as the basis of an appeal: 'I remind him that he expects me to do this when I'm busy.' This element of symmetry is, of course, implied in a 'personal' as against a 'positional' mode of relating between mother and child.

Mothers were asked about cheekiness on the part of the child. One would expect cheekiness to be more of an issue in positional families (since it implies relations of authority) so it is not surprising that the comparison of those who treat it lightly ('I laugh most of the time') with those who 'don't allow it' shows an association with the child's role-taking ($p < 0.05$).

The pressure exerted upon the child to *apologise* was also examined in relation to the role-taking. Overall the children who were forced to apologise tended to be slightly poorer at role-taking, but this was not significant. Again, though, it was the 'personal' quality of some of the answers that was interesting – mothers who were more concerned that their child *be* sorry rather than that he *say* sorry, and mothers who recognised the emotional difficulty of apology from the child's point of view, for instance: 'I do try to insist – sometimes she will but...it's not easy for her.' The small group of mothers giving answers of this type had children significantly better at role-taking than the others. The issue of symmetry arises again in Tom's mother's answer: 'Even when they were very tiny I've always apologised to them on every occasion when I've felt it necessary – if they hear me apologising they'll know that's the way one does it.'

At the end of the interview there were some rather general questions about strictness and about the mothers' ideas on bringing up children. Answers to these questions were divided into two groups on the basis of their specific comments in answer to these questions. The first group were typically positional answers specifying only things that children should not be or should not do, e.g. Alice's mother: 'I don't like cheeky or rude children and I won't have them swearing at me or hitting me', or Peter's mother: 'They ought not to be allowed to rule the house.' The second group were those who specified things the child is encouraged in, often rather abstractly specified (e.g. 'independence', 'freedom', 'being themselves', 'learning to live with people' etc.) or who remarked upon individual characteristics of their own children. Predictably, children of the latter group were significantly better role-takers than children of the former group ($p < 0.05$).

As with the discussion of the results of the teaching task, it may be argued that the statistical associations demonstrated are merely reflections of a more general pattern of association between social control strategies, social class, the child's IQ etc. If the social control measures discussed were strongly related to social class and to the child's IQ then it would be hardly surprising to find them related to the role-taking measure. In fact this does not appear to be the situation. The role-taking measure itself is statistically significantly correlated with the child's IQ but not with the principal social class index. Taking first, then, the question of how social control strategies are related to the child's IQ, it transpires that of the seven distinctions of control strategy shown in the preceding pages to be associated with the child's role-taking ability, only two also showed a significant degree of association with the child's IQ (smacking and concessions). Distinctions drawn in the handling of temper, apology, siblings quarrelling, cheekiness and in the mother's general comments were not significantly related to the child's IQ.

The 'personal' and 'positive' attitudes found to be associated with role-taking may conjure up an image of a middle class ideal of child-centeredness, but in fact within this sample these attitudes do not appear strongly related to social class. Using an admittedly crude dichotomy of the occupational status of the fathers (Classes I, II, III (white collar) vs III (manual) and IV) it was found that *none* of the distinctions in social control strategy were significantly associated with social class. It was noted in connection with the teaching task that the present sample is far from ideal for picking up social class differences. However it may also be noted that in the much larger scale study conducted by Cook-Gumperz (1973) in London, many of the expected social class differences were not demonstrated. She did find a significant association of physical punishment with social class, but the personal control categories of emotional support, concessions and bargaining were not found to be significantly class-related.

Negative findings in relation to IQ and social class do seem to add support to the argument that individual differences in role-taking ability are quite specifically associated with differences in style of interaction within the family, that these can usefully be characterised along a 'personal–positional' dimension, and that one way in which these are mediated to the child is through the means of social control employed in the family. Just as in the teaching task considered earlier, however, the interactional aspect of the situation cannot be ignored. The child's behaviour and personality may well influence the mother's use of, and attitude towards, various social control measures. We must therefore resist the temptation to adopt too simple a causal explanation of the present findings.

Perhaps the most striking feature of the range of the mothers' responses was the presence or absence of that element of symmetry which is implied by a 'personal' mode of relating between mother and child. One further example will be used to bring this out clearly: Kenneth's mother recounted a recent incident in which the child had fallen, fully clothed, into the bath while playing a game with a boat. His mother had burst out laughing, and the child threw a tantrum: 'He was terribly hurt. He felt a fool, that was the trouble, and he couldn't laugh it off. He got almost hysterical.' So his mother told Kenneth a long story about how *she* had fallen into a river once in even sillier circumstances. The strategy was successful: 'He's told his daddy about it now, so it's talkable about!'

In this example mother is literally putting herself in the child's position. This is reminiscent of Piaget's remark, that 'the social relation of reciprocity . . . gradually imposes itself as a form of equilibrium between individuals considering themselves as equals' (1960, p. 20). Piaget attributed the requisite 'equality' to the child's relationships with his peers, but here we see that the child's mother may treat him on terms of equality (a constructed equality) despite the obvious asymmetry of the mother–child relationship.

A summary

In this chapter various sources of data have been used to examine the general hypothesis that young children's role-taking abilities might be related to the form of social relationships within the family, and in particular to the relationship between the mother and the child. Our approaches to this analysis have drawn heavily on sociolinguistic conceptualisations. The mother's speech *to* the child (in the teaching situation) and her speech *about* the child (in the interview) have been examined in several ways.

Firstly, in the teaching situation, a number of aspects of the mother's instruction of her child were investigated in relation to the child's role-taking abilities. It appeared that, at least among the mother–son pairs, the mothers of good role-takers gave relatively more preliminary instruction to the child, this being associated with a short 'completion' time. For both sexes such mothers praised their children more and tended to let them get on with the task, once begun, until they themselves encountered difficulties. Some of these measures were also associated with the child's IQ and results were made more complex by the fact that the educational status of the mother was predictive of outcome for girls but not for boys.

In the second part of the chapter various aspects of social control were examined using interview material. This analysis rested largely on Bernstein's distinction between personal and positional styles of inter-action. Categories from Bernstein and Cook's social control coding frame were used as starting points. The frequency of use of personal rationales by the mother was positively related to the child's role-taking ability. As to actual control strategies, 'avoidance' (indexed by the handling of quarrelsome siblings), 'emotional support' (indexed by the handling of temper tantrums), and 'concessions' (indexed by the 'busy' question) were similarly associated with good role-taking. The opposite result was obtained for physical punishment, which was associated significantly with poor role-taking on the part of the children. Adept role-taking in the children was also associated with a permissive attitude to cheekiness, with the mother's recognition of apology as an emotive issue from the child's point of view, and with final comments from the mother bearing upon the development of the child as an individual. Only a minority of the differences examined were significantly related to the child's IQ and no clear social class relationships were apparent. In general, then, the findings on social control provide surprisingly clear support for the hypothesis outlined earlier.

The interview material highlighted the symmetry of relations which is perhaps the crucial feature of a personal (as opposed to a positional) relationship. As far as the development of role-taking is concerned, the importance of this is probably not that these children were granted more personal autonomy in the particular fields considered, but rather that they were in general thought of and treated by their mothers on a much more personal level. This point will be developed in the final chapter, while chapter 6 will try to place the role-taking abilities of the four year olds in the broader context of their earlier and later development.

6

Before and after

All the material considered so far has been drawn from the study of fifty-six children just after their fourth birthday. But the study of the children at four was just a part of a longitudinal project, and we have information relating to them from their birth almost up to their sixth birthday, when they were established in full time schooling. In this chapter some of the material relating to the children at earlier and later ages will be drawn into the emerging picture of the development of role-taking sensitivity.

The initial sample was selected to consist of babies born of medically 'low risk' pregnancies into intact families. Approximately seventy families were studied at the outset, the loss of some 20% of the sample by the age of four being due in large part to families moving out of the range of our follow up (the southern half of England). Such sample losses do introduce distortions, but it would perhaps not be sensible in any case to claim a high degree of 'representativeness' for a small sample drawn from one particular place at one particular time. Our concern must be to understand relationships within the sample, rather than to generalise from particular measures.

The research programme consisted in studies over the first year, followed by a study when the children were just over three, then the four year old study which has already been described in detail, and finally follow-ups at home and school when the children were aged $5\frac{1}{2}$–6 years. These pieces of research differed widely in their immediate objectives, and thus in the kinds of data collected. No attempt will be made to review them adequately here, since we are concerned only with their bearing on the issues raised in the preceding chapters.

Mother and baby in the first year

The importance for later social development of the early establishment of 'attachment' between mother and child has been widely accepted, the work of John Bowlby (1951, 1969) having been particularly influential. Mary Ainsworth has stressed the importance of the mother's sensitivity and responsiveness to the child in the formation of such attachments (Ainsworth and Bell, 1969; Ainsworth, Bell and Stayton, 1974). More recently there has been much interest in the possibility of a 'sensitive period' immediately after birth in which the mother is particularly open to the formation of a strong emotional bond with the child (Kennell, Trause and Klaus, 1975). So both in the immediate post-partum period and throughout the first year there is a suggestion that qualitative differences in adjustment and interaction between mother and baby may have important consequences for the developing relationship. The studies conducted with the present sample during the first year were in part concerned with obtaining measures of such adjustment and interaction.

The research was carried out by Martin Richards and Judy Bernal (now Dunn). Details of procedures are given in Richards and Bernal (1972) and Dunn (1975). Mothers were recruited to the sample before the birth of the child, and precoded delivery information was collected by the midwife. On days 2–10 observations of feeding sessions were made, and detailed diary information was obtained from the mothers. Visits were made at 8, 14, 20 and 30 weeks. One feeding session and two periods with the baby awake but not feeding were observed in the course of two visits at each age.

In the first ten day period there was little evidence of a simple unitary dimension of maternal warmth or sensitivity. Measures of how much the mother smiled at or looked at the baby were related to her 'affectionate talking' to the baby, but these were not related to her responsiveness to crying or to the amount of touching or caressing. These first ten day measures showed few significant relationships with the observations made between 8 and 30 weeks. Within the latter, however, they found consistent individual differences in the amount of touching, talking and responsiveness to vocalisations. There were also moderate positive correlations between these measures.

The lack of correlation between the first ten day coordination measures and later consistent maternal measures seems to suggest that the post-partum period, rather than being a particularly sensitive one, may actually be a period when the relationship between mother and child is buffered against difficulties of adjustment (Dunn, 1975). It does appear that after some weeks mother and baby settle to a characteristic pattern. This being so, we may wonder whether this pattern is particularly significant for (or predictive of) the subsequent social and cognitive development of the child. Bowlby's (1969) emphasis on the significance of early attachment would, as noted earlier, lead one to expect such relationships, and the claim has certainly been made that measures of attachment in the first year are predictive of future cognitive and linguistic development (e.g. Ainsworth, Bell and Stayton, 1974).

For half of the sample, hour-long audiotape recordings of mother–child interaction were obtained at 14 months. These were analysed in terms of Nelson's (1973) categories, which include measures of 'direction', 'acceptance' and 'rejection'. The observational measures from the 8 to 30 week visits (touching, talking, responsiveness to vocalisation etc.) showed no significant relationships with the 14 month verbal feedback indices from the tapes. Neither did the observational measures (which are typical of those examined under the attachment rubric in the first year) show any significant relationships to the Stanford–Binet IQ scores at four years of age or to the role-taking sensitivity measure obtained from the four year olds.

We therefore have no evidence of any straightforward continuity of relationship between attachment indices in the first year and later measures of reciprocity in verbal exchange or of the social and cognitive development of the child. This should perhaps lead us not simply to a denial of continuity, but to a reconsideration of the kinds of methods and measures employed (Richards, 1977). Lawrence Kohlberg has argued that the security aspects of the early relationship with the mother, particularly the proximity and physical contact which have been emphasised by attachment theorists, may actually be irrelevant to later social behaviour. He points out that while we see adult social relationships in terms of reciprocity, communication and cooperation, these features hardly enter into theories of attachment in infancy. He suggests that reciprocal play (as in the 'peekaboo' games studied by Bruner and Sherwood, 1975) may be much more pertinent to social development than, say, measures of affectionate touching or responsiveness to crying. If only in a negative fashion, the results of the analyses discussed in this section lend some support to Kohlberg's position.

Before leaving the first year material, it may be worth noting one other negative finding. All babies were rated at birth using a modified Apgar scale, giving ratings on three 3-point scales of colour, muscle tone and reflex irritability. About a quarter scored a total of seven points or less and these were referred to as the poor birth status group, although it should be emphasised that 'poor' in this case means only somewhat less than optimum. The poor birth status group has been shown to differ in a number of respects in the first three years (Barnes, 1975), including having a higher frequency of accidents and more sleep problems. However, the social role-taking measures at age four, which are the hub of our present considerations, showed absolutely no relationship to this index of birth status.

Social behaviour at three years of age
All the mothers were interviewed by Frances Barnes within a few weeks of the children's thrid birthdays. The interview was of an extended open-ended nature and was tape recorded. It resembled that used at four years (see Ch. 4) but was focussed less on discipline and parental control and more on the children's behaviour.

Questions relating to the children's social behaviour were examined in terms of possible relationships with social role-taking. We expected that the adept role-takers at four might have been more 'socially confident' a year earlier, and there was evidence of this. For example thirty-one of the children were described as being somewhat upset by strangers, or at least as needing time to 'warm up'. The remaining seventeen were described as being friendly towards strangers straight away. The latter group, at four, were significantly better role-takers ($p < 0.05$). Similarly, on a question asking about the child's behaviour in unfamiliar houses, twenty-nine were described as being upset or 'clinging' in this situation while the remaining fifteen were said to enjoy going into unfamiliar houses, and to explore freely from the beginning. The latter group, a year later, were significantly better role-takers ($p < 0.05$). Answers to a question about obedience and another about the mother's general view of how easy the child was to manage showed no significant relationship to later role-taking. With some exceptions to be considered later, the same is true of other questions relating to the non-social abilities and behaviour of the children.†

It appears, then, that the children who perform well on the role-taking

† It is interesting to note that a question on books did show a relationship approaching significance. Mothers were asked whether their child enjoyed books, either to look at himself or to have read to him. The small number (8) for whom a negative answer was given tended to be poorer role-takers at four ($p = 0.06$, one tailed), there being no relationship to IQ.

tasks at four tend, a year earlier, to be more confident with strangers, more confident in strange houses, and perhaps less frequently bored. Given the substantial intercorrelation of the role-taking scores with Stanford–Binet IQ at four, we looked to see whether any of these three year old interview measures were also significantly associated with IQ. None of them were, which suggests that the connections drawn are reasonably specific ones.

A card sorting technique was employed by Frances Barnes as an extension to the interview. The procedure paralleled that used in the individual form of the MMPI (Hathaway and McKinley, 1951). A set of cards, each of which bore a statement about the behaviour of a child, were sorted by the mothers according to whether the statement was true of their child or not. One of the cards described a child who 'always wants to be near his mother'. Children who at four were good role-takers tended not to be so classified ($p < 0.05$). Related to this, the description 'wants to help mother in her occupations around the house' was less often selected as true of the good role-takers ($p < 0.05$). This suggests an interpretation in terms of dependence and independence, the good role-takers being more independent of the mother in their play.

Children who would later be poor role-takers tended to be classified as finding difficulty in amusing themselves. This was not adequately significant statistically ($p < 0.1$) but is consistent with the interview finding concerning boredom. In line with the expectation of greater social confidence in the better role-takers, mothers of such children tended less often to classify them at three as 'not liking to be left with other people even if he knows them' ($p < 0.05$, one tailed). Of these card-sorts, none were significantly related to four year old IQ with the exception of 'wanting to help mother in her occupations around the house', where the relationship was similar to that shown with the role-taking score.

The less obviously social behaviours (feeding, tidiness, fussing about going to bed etc.) were not for the most part related to role-taking, but one rather unexpected relationship did emerge. The good role-takers were more frequently classified as often whining, fussing and shouting to get their own way ($p < 0.05$). Had this been an entirely isolated finding we would have ignored it, but it ties in with two other findings from the interview material at three. On a question about temper tantrums and bouts of bad behaviour the eight children for whom such occurrences were said to be frequent (more than four per week on average) were found to be significantly *better* role-takers at four. On a question about bowel and bladder control, 25 of the children were described as being completely clean and dry in the daytime, while the other 25 were having at least occasional 'accidents'. These less reliable children were better role-takers a year later ($p = 0.05$). There were also nonsignificant tendencies for good role-takers to have been fussy eaters and to have woken at night frequently.

To summarise these findings from the three year interview and card-sorting procedures, then, good role-taking a year later was associated with friendliness towards strangers, a willingness to be left in the care of others, and eagerness to explore novel surroundings. Adept role-takers tended at three to be rarely bored and not to depend heavily upon their mother's presence and her activities to support their play. However, on the negative side, good role-taking seems to have been associated with temper and bad behaviour, with the child shouting to get his own way, and with at least occasional daytime wetting or soiling. We shall return to this interesting pattern of relationships in later discussion.

Patterns of communication between three year olds and their mothers
Frances Barnes conducted another study with the three year olds in which she attempted to characterise the mother–child relationships from direct observation rather than interview data. The approach she adopted follows from the application of 'Systems Theory' to communicative interactions, and is outlined by Watzlawick, Beavin and Jackson (1968).

Two samples of communication were obtained from each mother–child pair. Firstly, a typical midday meal was observed and tape recorded, observations commencing when the child sat up to the table and terminating when he finally left the table. Secondly, on a separate occasion, the observer brought a box of toys, and asked the mother to play with the child for about ten minutes. Again conversations were tape recorded.

Categories for analysis of the tape transcripts were derived from Mark (1971). The analysis focusses upon the relationship between successive utterances. Mark distinguishes three 'meta-communicative' categories: confirmation (agreement), rejection (negation) and disconfirmation (non-existence of relationship). Where there is confirmation the second speaker agrees with, accepts, and possibly extends, the statement made by the first speaker. Rejection occurs when the second speaker disagrees, negates the first speaker's utterance, and possibly goes on to extend the negation by further comment. Given the issues raised in the last chapter, it was natural to look at the results of this analysis to see whether a high degree of confirmation (relative to rejection) characterised the children who at four were good role-takers. The ratio of confirmation to rejection provides an index of the extent of positive consensus and has the advantage of being independent of the length of the transcript.

The expectation that parents of good role-takers would show a higher ratio of confirmation to rejection of the child's utterances (a more 'positive' relationship – see chapter 5) was not confirmed. Although the differences were in the expected direction, the relationship with the role-taking scores was not significant either for the meal-time or the toy play observations. However, an examination of the child's confirmation or rejection of the parent's utterances showed that the children who were to be good role-takers at four produced a somewhat higher ratio of confirmation to rejection in the meal-time observations ($p = 0.07$, one tailed).† Although information on the toy play session was available for only about half the sample the same relationship was shown more clearly ($p < 0.05$, one tailed). We have some evidence, then, that adept role-taking at four is associated, a year earlier, with a relatively low level of disagreement with, or negation of, the mother's utterances by the child.

A more interesting category, perhaps, is 'disconfirmation'. This refers to a situation where one individual completely ignores something which another has said to him. While confirmation and rejection are seen as means of qualifying or modifying the relationship between two people, disconfirmation is taken as a denial of the existence of the relationship (Mark, 1971). The concept of disconfirmation has been used extensively in psychotherapy, and Laing (1961) has discussed at length the way in which disconfirmation may undercut the foundations of awareness of self and of other. There seems good reason, then, to expect a negative relationship between such disconfirmation and social role-taking.

From the tape transcripts the only kind of disconfirmation which can be identified reliably is the case where a statement has been made which demands a response from the other person, but where the latter 'replies' with a remark bearing no relationship to the first statement. Thus, for example, the child might say 'Can I have an apple?' and the mother might say 'Careful with those cups', making no further reference to the child's request. Amongst the meal-time transcripts 23 were identified where there were several clear instances of such disconfirmation. As hypothesised, these 23 children were significantly poorer role-takers a year later than

† This becomes highly significant statistically if the extreme group (more than twice as much agreement as disagreement) is compared with the remainder ($p < 0.01$, one tailed).

the remaining 21 ($p < 0.05$). The same picture was shown in the subsample for which toy-play transcripts were available, though here the relationship reaches significance only if a one tailed statistic is judged appropriate ($p < 0.05$, one tailed). Children's disconfirmations of their mothers' remarks were less common. Their relationship with the role-taking measure was in the same direction but was nonsignificant.

The child's IQ at four was not significantly related to any of the disconfirmation measures, nor was it related to the confirmation/rejection measure from the toy play. The confirmation/rejection measure from the meal-time was positively related to IQ at four ($p < 0.05$).

Before going on to consider these findings in a broader context, some results from the study of the children at the age of five and a half will be presented.

Social adjustment in the first year at school

A study of the social adjustment of the children towards the end of the first year in school was conducted by Barbara Antonis. Apart from the practical importance of the children's accommodation to school, this provided an opportunity of evaluating the children's behaviour outside the context of the home. The Bristol Social Adjustment Guide (Stott, 1971) was used to obtain systematic and reliable observations from the teachers involved. The BSAG is designed specifically to obtain information from teachers on the behaviour of children in the school context. The teacher is asked to underline phrases which describe the behaviour of the child – she is thus reporting observed behaviour rather than interpreting it. The scoring is in terms of five 'core syndromes' which are grouped under either Under-reacting (UNRACT) or Over-reacting (OVRACT) modes of maladjustment. Under UNRACT come Unforthcomingness, Depression and Withdrawal and under OVRACT come Inconsequence and Hostility.

The manual suggests a minimum period of teacher–child contact of about a month prior to the teacher completing the guide. In the present case, all of the children had been with the teacher completing the guide for at least a term. The children ranged from 5 years 6 months to 5 years 9 months when the guides were completed.

The BSAG was designed primarily to assess behaviour disturbances for clinical purposes, so not surprisingly in the present sample the numbers of children receiving sufficient scores to indicate significant maladjustment were small. One tailed statistics have been used in this section as there seem sufficient grounds, both theoretical (see Ch. 1) and empirical (see Ch. 2), for predicting the direction of the relationships involved.

Of the UNRACT groups the most reliable syndrome score is Unforthcomingness (Stott, 1971) and this was the only one for which sufficient data were available for separate analysis. Unforthcomingness is defined as apprehensiveness about facing new tasks or new situations, leading to withdrawn, apprehensive behaviour and a lack of initiative. Ten out of the 51 children for whom data are available obtained scores exceeding the suggested cut-off point and were thus classified as at least mildly maladjusted in this respect. We may predict that such apprehensiveness in new (and generally social) situations should be associated with poorer role-taking at four. This is indeed the case: the ten children classified as 'Unforthcoming' have significantly poorer role-taking scores than the remainder ($p < 0.05$). Scores on Withdrawal and Depression were too few to analyse separately, but on the UNRACT totals six children scored highly enough to be classified as 'appreciably maladjusted'. These six had scored significantly less well on role-taking at four ($p < 0.05$).

Of the OVRACT group the most reliable syndrome score is Inconsequence, defined as a failure to inhibit the first response which comes to mind, especially aggressive responses to frustration: 'The child acts impulsively without an advance mental rehearsal of the consequences [and] thus behaves in ways which are unsuitable or harmful or annoying to other people' (Stott, 1971, p. 11). For Mead, and to some extent for Piaget, such unreflective attitudes may be expected to go hand in hand with poor social role-taking (Ch. 1, pp. 7–14). The six children who exceeded the suggested criterion on Inconsequence had indeed scored significantly less well than the remainder on role-taking at four ($p < 0.05$). There were too few scorers under Hostility for this to be analysable, and on the OVRACT total score only one child was classified as appreciably maladjusted. It is perhaps worth noting that this child was the one who had scored the most poorly of all the 56 children on role-taking at four years. With an IQ at four of 109, he was by no means the lowest scorer on general intelligence. IQ was not significantly related either to Unforthcomingness or to the UNRACT total. There was a significant relationship between IQ and Inconsequence, which is perhaps not surprising given the definition of that syndrome.

Since the numbers of children obtaining significant maladjustment scores under the various headings is small, it may be that the relationships which have been uncovered hold only for an extreme group. Nevertheless the results do broadly suggest that the four year old role-taking measure is predictive of failures of adjustment in school some eighteen months later.

One other piece of information, gathered at the same time as the BSAG data, is perhaps worth mentioning here. The teachers were asked to rate the child's reading ability, simply as to whether it was above average, average or below. The 22 children rated as above average in reading had been substantially better role-takers at four ($p < 0.002$). Rather surprisingly, above average reading ability at five and a half was not significantly associated with IQ at four ($p = 0.11$).

A study of communication skills

Effective verbal communication has often been held to depend upon role-taking, since it requires the speaker to make adjustments in his message to suit the informational needs of his listener (e.g. Flavell, 1968). Participants in a communicative exchange must accommodate to one another's perspectives, and this makes role-taking central to the achievement of a smooth, effective exchange of information.

Barbara Antonis investigated communicative skills in a study conducted in the children's homes when they were between 5 years 6 months and 5 years 7 months of age. She adapted a technique used by Krauss and Glucksberg (1969, 1977). The child was asked to sit at one side of a table on which was a screen. On the other side of the screen was an adult, a confederate of the tester (who sat at one side of the table to observe and tape-record the proceedings). In the first task the child and the adult listener were each given six schematic pictures of heads and shoulders which differed from one another in three dimensions only. A picture could be uniquely specified by giving information on whether the mouth was smiling or not, whether the tie was striped or plain and whether the head had hair or not. After an initial matching task which assured that the child could discriminate the pictures accurately, he was asked to specify a given picture to the adult listener, and was given feedback of results. This was done for each picture and a 'total information score' was derived on the basis of the number of relevant details specified. The question which is important for us is whether the children identified as good role-takers were more able, in this situation, to select the relevant attributes for the listener. A highly significant relationship was found between the 'total information score' and four year old role-taking scores ($p < 0.005$). The total information score showed a positive but nonsignificant relationship to IQ ($p < 0.1$).

The second task employed less simplified materials, but was otherwise similar. The pictures were of trees and differed in a number of respects which were quite difficult to characterise verbally. The children used a variety of levels of description in this situation, and scoring depended upon whether the children succeeded in producing messages which enabled the listener to pick out the correct pictures each time. When they failed to do so, even after nonspecific encouraging remarks from the tester, they were given direct prompts (e.g. 'tell him about the leaves'). Only 12 of the 45 children tested at this stage got through the task without needing such prompts. These twelve were significantly better role-takers than the remainder on the basis of the four year old measures ($p < 0.01$). The relationship with IQ was again not quite significant ($p < 0.1$).

The third task was somewhat different, though it still employed the screen. The child and the adult listener both had a box containing mosaic pieces of various shapes and colours. The child was asked to copy a pattern which he was shown and then to tell the listener how to construct an identical pattern. The scoring depended upon whether the child specified the following aspects: numbers, shapes and colours of constituent items, contiguity of colours and of shapes, and overall shape. The total score based on this analysis was significantly related to the role-taking scores ($p < 0.005$) but in this instance was even more clearly related to IQ ($p < 0.0005$).

In the first task the problem was to pick out features which would enable the listener to discriminate amongst the faces. In the second task the problem was usually solved by finding a graphic, shareable image (e.g. 'a Christmas tree', 'a winter tree'). On both these tasks children's abilities were substantially related to their earlier role-taking abilities and not to a measure of general intelligence. In the mosaics task both these relationships were shown, perhaps because communication depended much more upon producing a technically correct description of a complex figure. A good description in this task required a complex coordination of information about the units and their spatial arrangement. These results, taken together, seem to support the view that differences in communication skill are associated with differences in role-taking ability, with the proviso that communication often makes demands on many other kinds of ability.

A very wide range of developmental phenomena have been considered in this chapter, ranging across the age range from birth to five. All have been treated from the point of view of what they tell us about the origins and consequences of individual differences in role-taking sensitivity. Rather than attempting a summary at this point we shall leave it to the next and final chapter to review and discuss these findings in the context of the study as a whole.

7

Reflections

In this final chapter an attempt will be made to summarise the main themes of earlier chapters and to draw together and comment upon some of the empirical findings.

At the outset we noted that, until recently, research on children's thinking has concentrated heavily upon reasoning and problem solving in relation to the physical as opposed to the social environment. It has been widely accepted, however, that social and nonsocial aspects of cognition must be intimately related.

Piaget, especially in his earlier writings, used the concept of egocentrism to draw together individual and social aspects of thinking. The egocentric child was held to 'center' on one aspect of an object or situation and in just the same way to 'center' on his own viewpoint in a social situation. The achievement of operational thinking was thus firmly linked to the overcoming of egocentrism. Since Piaget suggested that social experience was necessary for the latter process, it might seem that such experience must have a central role in the genesis of operational thinking. However, this aspect of his theory has received very little emphasis, and Piaget himself has made no real attempt to characterise the processes involved.

Until recently Piaget has not addressed himself to the question of the child's awareness of his own mental activity (Piaget, 1977). It has often been unclear how far he supposed the child to be capable of reflecting upon his own operatory thought. This question of awareness has a central place in the writings of G. H. Mead. The developmental phenomena in which Piaget saw the diminution of egocentrism and the progressive *socialisation* of thought, Mead (along with Vygotsky) saw as marking emerging self-awareness and the progressive *individualisation* of thought.

To a large extent this is a matter of seeing 'the other side of the same coin', of course. Mead went much further than Piaget toward viewing rationality as a social construct, developed by people collectively rather than individually, but the two theories have many fundamental similarities. In particular, Piaget's concept of egocentrism ties in very closely with Mead's emphasis on role-taking, and Kohlberg could have been paraphrasing either Mead or Piaget when he wrote that: 'The basic starting point of any analysis of the growth of social knowledge...must be the fact that all social knowledge implies...taking the viewpoint of another self or group of selves' (1969, p. 416).

Piaget and Inhelder's (1956) studies of visual perspective-taking seemed to show that children were not able to make accurate, nonegocentric predictions concerning another's point of view until at least seven or eight years of age. Many of the more recent studies, however, clearly point to the conclusion that preschool children are not profoundly egocentric. Children as little as two or three years old can manage certain very basic inferences about other people's viewpoints. As Shantz (1975) concludes from her review of this work, the preschooler has emerged as much more competent in his social understanding than we had given him credit for being.

The results from the role-taking tasks employed in the present study certainly demonstrate that four year olds are by no means totally egocentric. On the first orientation task, for example, 18 of the 56 children always oriented the figure correctly, while 16 oriented the figure egocentrically every time. The hiding games showed up a surprisingly high level of competence. In the second of them, for instance, over a third of the children eventually found the correct hiding place each time without directive prompting, showing that in very simple situations many of the children could not only establish what would and what would not be visible to another, they could also coordinate these perspectives.

The inclusion of a considerable number of tasks tapping visual perspective-taking was in part a response to Flavell's suggestion that this type of role-taking should be easier than that involving the cognitions, intentions or emotions of another. In practice it was clear that many of the tasks designed primarily as measures of visual perspective-taking elicited signs of role-taking (or the lack of it) in a much more general sense. This was especially true of the hiding tasks (pp. 49–55). On the penny-hiding task and the 'faces' task, moreover, many of the children displayed quite well developed sensitivity to the expectations and feelings of the other party. Scores on these tasks were substantially correlated with scores on the visual perspective-taking tasks.

Research in this area has very often been directed at the specification of 'ages and stages' in the development of role-taking ability (e.g. Selman, 1973; Flavell, 1974). However, a good deal of difficulty has been encountered in the attempts to apply simple models of successive stages. Tasks supposedly tapping the same levels of role-taking may produce widely differing performances, and apparently minor details of task design or of response requirement often seem to make a great deal of difference to the difficulty of the task (eg. Weinheimer, 1972; Eiser, 1977). There is a tendency to assume that differences in group performance between different tasks, and differences in individual performance on any one task, must directly reflect the presence or absence of competence for a particular level of role-taking inference. But a number of authors (e.g. Flavell, 1974; Levine and Hoffman, 1975) have suggested that there may in fact be a considerable gap between the availability of the inferential skills involved and the spontaneous *use* of such skills in any given situation.

Indeed if we accept the evidence of the recent studies mentioned in chapter 2 we might reasonably conclude that all of the children tested in the present study should have had the requisite competence to succeed on all of the tasks. They manifestly did not do so, and it is with the individual differences in success and failure that we have been mainly concerned. If a distinction is made between competence and performance, then, our emphasis has been on the latter. Individual differences have been construed as being governed by the degree of sensitivity shown by the child to the role-taking requirements of a given situation. Acredolo (1977) stresses the effectiveness of prompting on the spatial perspective-taking performance of four year olds, and it is probably of some significance that the detailed scoring of many of our tasks was dependent upon the extent to which such prompting was necessary.

The matrices of correlation and partial correlation presented in chapter 4 show that scores on the role-taking tasks are significantly intercorrelated, and that they remain so even after allowing for the children's IQ. The correlations average about $+0.4$, and a principal components analysis gave a first component accounting for approximately half of the total variance. In the discussion of this analysis it was suggested that the second (and perhaps subsequent) components might best be interpreted in terms of the particular forms of role-taking inferences required by the various tasks, or the particular difficulties of application of such inferences in each type of task (Ch. 4, p. 71). What, then, are we to make of the large first component? What have tasks such as these (ranging from 'orientation' to 'penny-hiding', from 'interposition' to 'faces') in common? The preceding paragraphs suggest an answer, namely that if the common variance is to be seen in role-taking terms at all then it should be seen as a reflection of the child's general level of *awareness* of perspective differences and of the need to adapt to them.

The adoption of this emphasis on awareness or sensitivity brings us much closer to role-taking differences as we understand them amongst adults. A certain piece of adult behaviour may be construed as egocentric (i.e. as reflecting a failure to see another's point of view) without it being implied that the adult concerned lacks knowledge of the existence of perspective differences, or is *incapable* of taking account of them. In children, just as in adults, it may be more appropriate, for some purposes, to treat role-taking as a disposition or 'habit of thinking' rather than as a series of quasi-logical acquisitions. This approach naturally undermines attempts at a structural analysis in terms of stages. Indeed it suggests that the same kinds of things which govern individual differences amongst young children may govern comparable individual differences in adulthood.

Using a simple total score from the eight role-taking tasks, characteristics of the children and their families were investigated in order to discover some of the concomitants of the marked individual differences in role-taking. To some extent IQ has been used as a crude 'control' measure, interest centering on those relationships with the role-taking measure which are not accountable for by reference to shared dependence on 'general intelligence'. In as far as the correlates of the role-taking measure have confirmed theoretical predictions and commonsense expectations they have been used to lend validity to that measure. At the same time such validity has been assumed in the attempt to extend existing knowledge concerning the development of role-taking sensitivity. The validation requirement is conceptually prior, but in practice all the results contribute to the validation, and the interpretation of those results must be contingent upon the validation provided by the study as a whole.

In chapter 2 a variety of suggestions concerning the kinds of social interaction which might be particularly important for the development of role-taking sensitivity were considered. Some relevant evidence was presented in chapter 4, although perhaps the main conclusion to be drawn from it is that the picture is more complex than has commonly been supposed, and that relatively crude quantitative measures are not very revealing. Evidence from the 'standard day' interviews tended to confirm the suggestions of Kohlberg, Flavell and others regarding the importance of close ('concentrated') adult attention. Piaget's emphasis on the importance of social contact with peers was not supported, in that the children who spent most time with their peers did not appear to be the best role-takers. At this age solitary play appeared to be important, and children who spent most of their time with other children spent relatively little time in solitary play. Expectations concerning the relationships between role-taking and those aspects of the child's play stressed in Mead's writings were largely confirmed.

There is much that is unclear about how role-taking, in the sense in which we have used the term, is related to everyday social interaction. Even if one accepts that social interaction must be heavily dependent upon social role-taking, one is not bound to accept that the continous flow of largely unconsidered social adjustments can be reduced to, or approximated by, a series of role-taking tasks such as we have used here. Moreover it is by no means clear what aspects of social behaviour we should expect to be associated with adept role-taking. The available experimental literature gives little insight into the relation between social cognition and social behaviour. In her review Shantz (1975) noted the lack of evidence on the ways in which specific types of social interaction influence children's social understanding, or vice versa. The least equivocal evidence on this issue concerns the relationship between poor role-taking and emotional disturbance and delinquency (Ch. 2, pp. 30–1). However, the relevant studies have typically been conducted with selected 'critical groups' of children considerably older than those in the 'normal' sample studied here.

While none of our four year olds had been classified as clinically disturbed (or delinquent!) it was nonetheless possible to look at role-taking in relation to the limited information on cooperativeness and sharing, temper and aggressiveness obtained from the maternal interview. No significant relationships were found.

Rather more detailed information on social behaviour and adjustment was available at earlier and later ages. The children who at four were good role-takers showed the following characteristics at three. They were more friendly towards strangers, more willing to be left in the care of others, and more confident in novel surroundings. They were less heavily dependent upon the mother's presence to support their activities and were rarely bored. However, good role-taking also seemed to be associated with temper and bad behaviour, with the child fussing to get his own way, and with relatively unreliable toilet training.

The analysis of the Bristol Social Adjustment Guide material, obtained from the schools when the children were aged five and a half to five years nine months, lent some support to the association of poor role-taking with maladjustment. The relatively small numbers of children obtaining substantial maladjustment scores had been significantly poorer role-takers than the remainder at four.

For the most part, then, these relationships are consistent with sensitive role-takers being socially confident and accommodating easily to new relationships and new social situations such as the school. But the observation that at three certain 'negative' behaviours were more frequent amongst such children came as more of a surprise. Evidence reviewed in chapter 2 (pp. 30–1) does perhaps suggest that a positive association between 'pro-social' behaviours and role-taking is easier to establish for older children than for preschoolers, but it contains no suggestion of a *negative* relationship in the preschool years.†

It would be rash to give much weight to present findings on this point, especially since we have not attempted a structural analysis of relationships within the three year interview and card-sort data. Nonetheless they deserve comment. One possible interpretation would be that tantrums, occasional wetting and so on are just the kinds of behaviours which three year olds are learning to use as devices for manipulating others. This explanation treats such behaviours as social acts, with social consequences, rather than simply as evidencing a failure of socialisation. Speculative and *post hoc* though such an explanation may be, it at least serves as a reminder that we have no particularly good grounds for supposing that any behavioural correlates of role-taking should necessarily be socially desirable ones. For example, although we have no information on behaviours such as taunting or teasing, it would not be surprising to find that these were positive correlates of role-taking, since one has to be sensitive to the vulnerability of another in order to exploit it. The same applies in the adult world, of course. Perhaps the most obvious example is the 'confidence trickster', who relies for his success upon his ability to predict and deceitfully manipulate the beliefs and expectations of others. Role-taking is clearly no panacea, either for the problems of childrearing or for the ills of society!

† The one partial exception to this is a study by Feshbach and Feshbach (1969).

Central to this study has been the question of the relationship between the role-taking sensitivity of the child and the quality of the mother–child relationship. Flavell, Kohlberg and others (see Ch. 2, pp. 27–8) have suggested that the pattern of social interaction in the child's family may be crucial for role-taking development. Moreover it seems to follow from Mead's theory that this should be so. A number of approaches to this question were described in chapters 5 and 6.

The structured teaching task (pp. 83–8) served to establish certain interesting relationships between the ways in which the mothers instructed their children and the children's role-taking scores. However, the teaching task represents an artificial, contrived situation, and may be more 'artificial' for some mothers than for others. Some may be quite used to adopting such an instructional role with their children, others may not. The differences observed are therefore best treated only as indirect indicators of differences in relationship.

The same considerations apply to the interview material on social control, used to gain insight into the 'personal' quality of the mother–child relationship (pp. 88–94). The kinds of things the mothers said about their children, or about their own behaviour, may not have corresponded directly with what went on in the family. Nevertheless a consistent pattern of relationships emerged between how the mothers answered the questions and how well the children performed on the role-taking tasks. The prediction that a high degree of role-taking sensitivity should be related to a highly 'personal' maternal style was clearly supported. Cook-Gumperz specifically says of personal control that, 'in the Meadian sense, it encourages reflexiveness' (1973, p. 202). The fact that we have been able to show relationships between aspects of personal control and the child's role-taking sensitivity lends support to this claim and thus indirectly to Mead's general theoretical position.

In the first chapter the significance of 'the child in the eyes of his mother' was discussed in relation to Mead's theory of the development of self-knowledge and self-awareness. The importance of the mother's view of the child has been heavily stressed more recently by Shotter (1974). Shotter sees the very young child as essentially unreflective, and he argues that the concepts which the mother has of the child, in terms of which she interacts with him, are of vital importance in helping the child to get beyond his initially unreflective condition. To achieve this, he argues, the child must be treated as 'a full term in a personal relationship' (1974, p. 223).

Many of the things shown in chapter 5 to be related to the child's role-taking sensitivity can be conceptualised in terms of whether the mother acted towards, or spoke of, the child *as a person*. The 'symmetry' noted in relation to some of the answers to interview questions did not imply that the child was treated as an adult rather than as a child. It implied that he was treated as an autonomous individual, possessed of his own thoughts and feelings, his own likes and dislikes, and so on. A common feature of 'personal' rationales and control strategies seemed to be the implicit recognition that the child's behaviour could be interpreted in terms of underlying motives and intentions, or in terms of an underlying *character* which the child possesses for good or ill, and which constitutes him as a person. In this sense, of course, one may see such personal control as an indication of the role-taking sensitivity of the mother.

Our restriction of attention to the child and his mother, to the exclusion of the father and other significant people in the child's life, represents an obvious limitation on the study. The fact that clear relationships have emerged between the mother's behaviour and attitudes and the child's role-taking does not necessarily indicate that the mother's role is crucial. It might be the case that the mother's behaviour and attitudes are a good guide to those of others with whom the child has contact. Such concordance might be thought to operate at the level of the individual family, as Bearison and Cassel suggest: 'Our interpretation...is that the mothers' responses reflected the shared standards of inter-personal behaviour that are practiced by all members of the family. Standards that are implicitly maintained by members of a person-oriented family constitute a psychological reality that is different in form from that realised in a position-oriented family' (1975, p. 36).

Alternatively, concordance might be seen in terms of wider socio-economic groupings. Clearcut social class differences have not been shown in the present study, either in the measures of maternal interaction styles or in the role-taking measure itself. While a larger and more broadly based sample might well show up such differences, it is clear that there is a great deal of variation between families which is not 'accountable for' in terms of social class.

Interesting questions obviously arise concerning the determinants of this variation, but we must leave them largely unanswered for the present. We cannot ignore the role of the child himself in the establishment of his mother's behaviour towards him. Their interaction must have the form of a negotiation, and individual characteristics of the child must contribute to 'the sort of child his mother sees him as being'. The frequency with which the mothers in this study commented on differences in the characters of their several children seemed to confirm this. However, it is just this kind of individuality to which a highly 'person-oriented' mother will be sensitive, so that she will treat her children very differently according to how she sees their emotional needs. We have, then, to differentiate between a mother's disposition to be responsive to her children 'as persons' on the one hand, and the particular way she comes to see a given child on the other. The interactive basis of the latter is clear, while the former may reflect a fairly stable aspect of the mother's personality.

Some data on earlier mother–child interaction were examined in chapter 6. Observational material from the first year of the child's life was not found to be at all predictive of role-taking sensitivity at four. It may be that there *is* no continuity, or it may be that the measures obtained (Ch. 6, pp. 97–9) related too much to the proximity and security aspects of early attachment and too little to the eaarly development of social reciprocity.

The study of conversations between mothers and three year olds (pp. 101–3) did bring to light some significant relationships with later role-taking. Poor role-taking at four was associated, a year earlier, with a relatively high level of disconfirmation of the child's utterances by the mother. Poor role-taking was also associated with a relatively high level of negation of the mother's utterances by the child, though not vice versa. While these findings are no more than suggestive, the approach adopted for analysis of mother–child interchanges seems a promising one for any future study of the patterns of relationship productive of role-taking sensitivity.

What of the relationship between role-taking and other aspects of the child's cognitive development. In the first chapter we considered two main accounts of the relationships involved. Piaget has argued that there is an isomorphism of the logical competences underlying reversible social relations and reversible concrete operations. Mead saw the relationship between these two in terms of a capacity for 'detached' or reflective thinking, a capacity achieved specifically through social experience. Mead's account suggests a reinterpretation of Piaget's 'concrete operations' in terms of developing self awareness and individual autonomy. This kind of reinterpretation seems to be implicit in much of the recent work on cognitive development in this period. It was indeed made explicit in a conclusion which McGarrigle and Donaldson drew from their fascinating study of conservation: 'It is possible that the achievements of the concrete operational stage are as much a reflection of the child's increasing independence from features of the interactional setting as they are evidence of the development of a logical competence' (1975, p. 349).

There is a sense, of course, in which any tests which we carry out with children can be seen as role-taking tests. The test situation is an 'interactional setting' within which the child has to try to understand what is required of him by the tester. This point was made in relation to the IQ test in chapter 4 (p. 70). It makes the establishment of the 'discriminant validity' of role-taking test very difficult, since it is not possible to find a test which makes no demands upon role-taking. Nevertheless we can conceptually distinguish the tests used in the present study as requiring 'doubly embedded' role-taking – they are role-taking tasks within a role-taking setting. In practice the statistical findings support a distinction between these tasks and the wide variety of others which go to make up the IQ test.

Apart from presenting some evidence that role-taking at four is predictive of later communication skills, and perhaps reading ability, we have not directly addressed the question of the relationship between role-taking and other aspects of cognition in the present study. If we have provided support for Mead's position on this question, it is by establishing a case for the argument that observed differences in role-taking are due, at least in part, to different kinds of social experience within the family. To this extent our findings contradict the alternative argument that role-taking is simply a manifestation in the social sphere of general processes of individual cognitive development.

Role-taking seems, then, to have fulfilled some of its promise as a concept which bridges social and individual aspects of cognition, and the way is open for much more detailed and delicate study of the relationship between cognitive development and experience in a social environment. Urie Bronfenbrenner, reviewing studies of the effectiveness of early intervention programmes aimed at overcoming the effects of early 'disadvantage' or 'deprivation', concluded that the involvement of the family as an active participant is crucial to the success of any intervention programme: 'It is as if the child himself had no way of internalising the processes which foster his growth, whereas the parent–child system does possess this capability' (1974, p. 54).

If the research presented in this volume has any contribution to make to wider issues in cognitive development, it is because it provides some guide to the factors which influence the achievement by the child of just such a 'way of internalising the processes which foster his growth'.

REFERENCES

Acredolo, L. (1977) 'Developmental changes in the ability to coordinate perspectives of a large scale space'. *Developmental Psychology*, **13**, 1–8.

Ainsworth, M. and Bell, S. (1969) 'Some contemporary patterns of mother–infant interactions in the feeding situation'. In Ambrose, A. (ed.) *Stimulation in Early Infancy*. London: Academic Press.

Ainsworth, M., Bell, S. and Stayton, D. (1974) 'Infant-mother attachment and social development'. In Richards, M. (ed.) *The Integration of a Child into a Social World*. Cambridge: The University Press.

Ambron, S. and Irwin, D. (1975) 'Role-taking and moral judgement in five- and seven-year-olds'. *Developmental Psychology*, **11**, 102.

Baldwin, T., McFarlane, P. and Garvey, C. (1971) 'Children's communication accuracy related to race and socioeconomic status'. *Child Development*, **42**, 345–57.

Barnes, F. (1975) 'Accidents in the first three years of life'. *Child: care, health and development*, **1**, 421–33.

Bearison, D. and Cassel, T. (1975) 'Cognitive decentration and social codes: communicative effectiveness in young children from differing family contexts'. *Developmental Psychology*, **11**, 29–36.

Bee, H., Van Egeren, L., Streissguth, A., Nyman, B. and Leckie, M. (1969) 'Social class differences in maternal teaching strategies and speech patterns'. *Developmental Psychology*, **1**, 726–34.

Berger, P. and Luckmann, T. (1967) *The Social Construction of Reality*. London: Allen Lane.

Berner, E. (1971) 'Private speech and role-taking abilities in preschool children'. Paper read to the biennial meeting of the Society for Research in Child Development, Minneapolis.

Bernstein, B. (1965) 'A socioloinguistic approach to social learning'. In Gould, J. (ed.) *Social Science Survey*. Harmondsworth: Penguin Books.

– (1970) 'A sociolinguistic approach to socialisation, with some reference to educability'. In Gumperz, J. and Hymes, D. (eds.) *Directions in Sociolinguistics*. New York: Holt, Rinehart and Winston.

– (1972) 'Social class, language and socialisation'. In Giglioli, P. (ed.) *Language and Social Context*. Harmondsworth: Penguin Books.

Bernstein, B. and Cook, J. (1968) 'Coding grid for maternal control'. Available from Dept. of Sociology, University of London, Institute of Education.

Borke, H. (1971) 'Interpersonal perception of young children: egocentrism or empathy?' *Developmental Psychology*, **5**, 263–9.

– (1972) 'Chandler and Greenspan's "Ersatz Egocentrism": a rejoinder'. *Developmental Psychology*, **7**, 107–9.

– (1973) 'The development of empathy in Chinese and American children between 3 and 6 years of age'. *Developmental Psychology*, **9**, 102–8.

Bowlby, J. (1946) *Forty-four Juvenile Thieves: their characters and home life.* London: Bailliere, Tindall and Cox.

– (1951) *Maternal Care and Mental Health.* Geneva: World Health Organisation.

– (1969) *Attachment and Loss*, Vol. 1, *Attachment.* London: Hogarth Press.

Brandis, W. and Henderson, D. (1970) *Social Class, Language and Communication.* London: Routledge and Kegan Paul.

Bronfenbrenner, U. (1974) *A Report on Longitudinal Evaluations of Pre-school Programs*, Vol. 2, *Is Early Intervention Effective?* Washington DC: DHEW Publication (OHD) 74–25.

Brophy, J. (1970) 'Mothers as teachers of their own preschool children: the influence of SES and task structure on teaching specificity'. *Child Development*, **41**, 79–94.

Bruner, J. and Sherwood, V. (1975) 'Early rule structure: the case of peekaboo'. In Bruner, J., Jolly, Q. and Sylva, K. (eds.) *Play: its role in evolution and development.* Harmondsworth: Penguin Books.

Bryant, P. (1974) *Perception and Understanding in Young Children.* London: Methuen.

Butler, N. and Bonham, D. (1963) *Perinatal Mortality.* Edinburgh and London: Livingstone.

Butterworth, G. and Cochran, E. (1978) 'Seeing eye to eye: towards a mechanism of joint visual reference'. Unpublished MS, Dept. of Psychology, University of Southampton.

Chandler, M. (1972) 'Egocentrism in normal and pathological child development'. In Monks, F., Hartup, W. and De Wit, J. (eds.) *Determinants of Behavioural Development.* London: Academic Press.

– (1973) 'Egocentrism and antisocial behaviour: the assessment and training of social perspective-taking skills'. *Developmental Psychology*. **9**, 326–32.

Chandler, M. and Greenspan, S. (1972) ' "Ersatz Egocentrism": a reply to Borke', H. *Developmental Psychology*, **7**, 104–6.

Chandler, M., Greenspan, S. and Barenboim, C. (1974) 'Assessment and training of role-taking and referential communication skills in institutionalised emotionally disturbed children'. *Developmental Psychology*, **10**, 546–53.

Coie, J., Costanzo, P. and Farnhill, D. (1973) 'Specific transitions in the development of spatial perspective-taking ability'. *Developmental Psychology*, **9**, 167–77.

Coie, J. and Dorval, B. (1973) 'Sex differences in the intellectual structure of social interaction skills'. *Developmental Psychology*, **8**, 261–7.

Cook-Gumperz, J. (1973) *Social Control and Socialisation.* London: Routledge and Kegan Paul.

Cox, M. (1975) 'The other observer in a perspectives task'. *British Journal of Educational Psychology*, **45**, 83–5.

Deutch, F. (1974) 'Observational and sociometric measures of peer popularity and their relationship to egocentric communication in female preschoolers'. *Developmental Psychology*, **10**, 745–7.

Deutch, F. and Stein, A. (1972) 'The effects of personal responsibility and task interruption on the private speech of preschoolers'. *Human Development*, **15**, 310–24.

De Vries, R. (1970) 'The development of role-taking as reflected by the behaviour of bright, average and retarded children in a social guessing game'. *Child Development*, **41**, 759–70.

Douglas, J., Lawson, A., Cooper, J. and Cooper, E. (1968) 'Family interaction and the activities of young children'. *Journal of Child Psychology and Psychiatry*, **9**, 157–71.

Dunn, J. (1975) 'Consistency and change in styles of mothering'. In *Parent–Infant Interaction*. Ciba Foundation Symposium, **33** (new series), Amsterdam: Elsevier.

Eiser, C. (1977) 'Strategies children use to coordinate perspectives as a function of task demands'. *British Journal of Educational Psychology*, **47**, 327–9.

Feshbach, N. and Feshbach, S. (1969) 'The relationship between empathy and aggression in two age groups'. *Developmental Psychology*, **1**, 102–7.

Fishbein, H., Lewis, S. and Keiffer, K. (1972) 'Children's understanding of spatial relations: coordination of perspectives'. *Developmental Psychology*, **7**, 21–33.

Flavell, J. (1963) *The Developmental Psychology of Jean Piaget*. Princetown, New Jersey: Van Nostrand.

– (1968) in collaboration with Botkin, P., Fry, C., Wright, J. and Jarvis, P. *The Development of Role-Taking and Communication Skills in Children*. New York: Wiley.

– (1974) 'The development of inferences about others'. In Mischel, T. (ed.) *Understanding Other Persons*, Oxford: Blackwell.

– Garner, J., Percy, L. and Lawson, T. (1971) 'Sex differences in behavioural impulsivity and attainment in young children'. *Journal of Child Psychology and Psychiatry*, **12**, 261–71.

Garvey, C. and Hogan, R. (1973) 'Social speech and social interaction: egocentrism revisited'. *Child Development*, **44**, 562–8.

Gottman, J., Gonso, J. and Rasmussen, B. (1975) 'Social interaction, social competence and friendship in children'. *Child Development*, **46**, 709–18.

Harré, R. and Secord, P. (1972) *The Explanation of Social Behaviour*. Oxford: Basil Blackwell.

Hartup, W. (1970) 'Peer interaction and social organisation'. In Mussen, P. (ed.) *Carmicheal's Manual of Child Psychology*, Vol. 2, New York: Wiley.

Hathaway, S. and McKinley, J. (1951) *Minnesota Multiphasic Personality Inventory Manual*. New York: The Psychological Corporation.

Heider, E. (1971) 'Style and accuracy of verbal communications within and between social classes'. *Journal of Personality and Social Psychology*, **18**, 33–47.

Hess, R. and Shipman, V. (1965) 'Early experience and the socialisation of cognitive modes in children'. *Child Development*, **36**, 869–86.

– (1972) 'Parents as teachers: how lower class and middle class parents teach'. In Lavatelli, C. and Stendler, F. (eds.) *Readings in Child Behaviour and Development* (3rd edn). New York: Harcourt, Brace, Jovanovich.

Hess, R., Shipman, V., Brophy, J. and Bear, R. (1969) 'The cognitive environments of urban preschool children: summary of the completed project'. Graduate School of Education, University of Chicago (unpublished paper).

Hoffman, M. (1970) 'Moral development'. In Mussen, P. (ed.) *Carmicheal's Manual of Child Psychology*, Vol. 2, New York: Wiley.

Hollos, M. (1975) 'Logical operations and role-taking abilities in two cultures: Norway and Hungary'. *Child Development*, 46, 638–49.

Hollos, M. and Cowan, P. (1973) 'Social isolation and cognitive development: logical operations and role-taking abilities in three Norwegian social settings'. *Child Development*, 44, 630–41.

Hoy, E. (1974) 'Measurement of egocentrism in children's communication'. *Developmental Psychology*, 11, 392.

Hughes, M. (1975) 'Egocentrism in Preschool Children'. Unpublished PhD thesis, University of Edinburgh.

Huttenlocher, J. and Presson, C. (1973) 'Mental rotation and the perspective problem'. *Cognitive Psychology*, 4, 277–99.

Ingleby, D. and Lawson, A. (1971) 'Some empirical results from the "standard day" interview technique'. In *Family interaction and the activities of young children*. Internal report, MRC unit on Environmental Factors in Mental and Physical Illness, London School of Economics.

Inhelder, B. and Piaget, J. (1958) *The Growth of Logical Thinking from Childhood to Adolescence*. New York: Basic Books.

James, W. (1904a) 'Does consciousness exist?' *Journal of Philosophy, Psychology and Scientific Methods*, 1, 477–91.

– (1904b) 'The pragmatic method'. *Journal of Philosophy, Psychology and Scientific Method*, 1, 673–87.

Jennings, K. (1975) 'People versus object orientation, social behaviour and intellectual abilities in preschool children'. *Developmental Psychology*, 11, 511.

Johnson, D. (1975) 'Affective perspective-taking and cooperative predisposition'. *Developmental Psychology*, 11, 869–70.

Kagan, J., Rosman, B., Day, D., Albert, J. and Phillips, W. (1964) 'Information processing in the child: significance of analytic and reflective attitudes'. *Psychological Monographs*, 78, No. 1.

Kennell, J., Trause, M. and Klaus, M. (1975) 'Evidence for a sensitive period in the human mother'. In *Parent–Infant Interaction*. Ciba Foundation Symposium, 33 (new series), Amsterdam: Elsevier.

Kohlberg, L. (1969) 'Stage and sequence: the cognitive-developmental approach to socialisation'. In Goslin, D. (ed.) *Handbook of Socialisation: Theory and Research*. New York: Rand McNally.

Kohlberg, L., Yaeger, J. and Hjertholm, E. (1968) 'Private speech: four studies and a review of theories'. *Child Development*, 39, 691–737.

Krauss, R. and Glucksberg, S. (1969) 'The development of communication competence as a function of age'. *Child Development*, 40, 255–66.

– (1977) 'Social and non-social speech'. In *Scientific American*, 236, 100–6.

Kurdek, L. and Rodgon, M. (1975) 'Perceptual, cognitive and affective perspective-taking in Kindergarten through sixth grade children'. *Developmental Psychology*, 11, 643–50.

Laing, R. D. (1961) *The Self and Others*. London: Tavistock.

Langer, J. (1969) *Theories of Development*. New York: Holt, Rinehart and Winston.

Lawson, A. and Ingleby, J. (1974) 'The daily routines of preschool children'. *Psychological Medicine*, 4, 399–415.

Lempers, J., Flavell, E. and Flavell, J. (1977) 'The development in very young children of tacit knowledge concerning visual perception'. *Genetic Psychology Monographs*, 95, 3–53.

Levine, L. and Hoffman, M. (1975) 'Empathy and cooperation in four year olds'. *Developmental Psychology*, 11, 533–4.

McGarrigle, J. and Donaldson, M. (1975) 'Conservation accidents'. *Cognition*, 3, 341–50.

Macmurray, J. (1957) *The Self as Agent*. London: Faber and Faber.

Maratsos, M. (1973) 'Nonegocentric communication abilities in preschool children'. *Child Development*, 44, 697–700.

Mark, R. (1971) 'Coding communication at the relationship level'. *Journal of Communication*, 21, 221–32.

Masangkay, Z., McCluskey, K., McIntyre, C., Sims-Knight, J., Vaughan, B. and Flavell, J. (1974) 'The early development of inferences about the visual percepts of others'. *Child Development*, 45, 357–66.

Masters, J. and Wellman, H. (1974) 'The study of human infant attachment: a procedural critique'. *Psychological Bulletin*, 81, 218–37.

Mead, G. H. (1934) *Mind, Self and Society*. Morris, C. W. (ed.) Chicago: University of Chicago Press.

Meltzer, B. (1967) 'Mead's social psychology'. In Manis, J. and Meltzer, B. (eds.) *Symbolic Interaction*. Boston: Allyn and Bacon.

Miller, D. (1973) *George Herbert Mead: Self, Language and the World*. Austin, Texas: University of Texas Press.

Mossler, D., Marvin, R. and Greenberg, M. (1976) 'Conceptual perspective taking in two to six year olds'. *Developmental Psychology*, 12, 85–6.

Mueller, E. (1972) 'The maintenance of verbal exchanges between young children'. *Child Development*, 43, 930–8.

Nahir, H. and Yussen, S. (1977) 'The performance of Kibbutz and city reared Israeli children on two role-taking tasks'. *Developmental Psychology*, 13, 450–5.

Neale, J. (1966) 'Egocentrism in Institutionalised and Non-institutionalised children'. *Child Development*, 37, 97–101.

Nelson, K. (1973) 'Structure and strategy in learning to talk'. *Monographs of the Society for Research in Child Development*, 38, Nos. 1–2.

Newson, J. and Newson, E. (1968) *Four Years Old in an Urban Community*. London: Allen and Unwin.

Nigl, A. and Fishbein, H. (1974) 'Perception and conception in coordination of perspectives'. *Developmental Psychology*, 10, 858–66.

Nunnally, J. (1967) *Psychometric Theory*. New York: McGraw Hill.

Olim, E. (1970) 'Maternal language styles and cognitive development of children'. In Williams, F. (ed.) *Language and Poverty*. Chicago: Markham.

Piaget, J. (1926) *The Language and Thought of the Child*. London: Routledge and Kegan Paul.

– (1928) *Judgement and Reasoning in the Child*. New York: Harcourt, Brace.

– (1932) *The Moral Judgement of the Child*. London: Routledge and Kegan Paul.

- (1950) *The Psychology of Intelligence*. London: Routledge and Kegan Paul.
- *The Construction of Reality in the Child*. London: Routledge and Kegan Paul.
- (1960) 'The general problems of the psychobiological development of the child.' In Tanner, J. and Inhelder, B. *Discussions on Child Development*, Vol. 4, London: Tavistock.
- (1965) *Etudes Sociologiques*. Geneva: Librarie Droz.
- (1970) Piaget's theory. In Mussen, P. (ed.) *Carmicheal's Manual of Child Psychology*, Vol. 1, New York: Wiley.
- (1971) *Structuralism*. London: Routledge and Kegan Paul.
- (1977) *The Grasp of Consciousness*. London: Routledge and Kegan Paul.
Piaget, J. and Inhelder, B. (1956) *The Child's Conception of Space*. London: Routledge and Kegan Paul.
- (1969) *The Psychology of the Child*. London: Routledge and Kegan Paul.
Piché, G., Michlin, M., Rubin, D. and Johnson, F. (1975) 'Relationships between fourth graders' performances on selected role-taking tasks and referential communication accuracy tasks'. *Child Development*, 46, 965–9.
Pufall, P. (1975) 'Egocentrism in spatial thinking'. *Developmental Psychology*, 11, 297–303.
Richards, M. (1977) 'Interaction and the concept of development revisited'. In Lewis, M. and Rosenblum, L. (eds.) *Interaction, Conversation and the Development of Language*. New York: John Wiley.
Richards, M. and Bernal, J. (1972) 'An observational study of mother–infant interaction'. In Blurton Jones, N. (ed.) *Ethological Studies of Child Behaviour*. Cambridge: The University Press.
Rothenberg, B. (1970) 'Children's social sensitivity and the relationship to interpersonal competence, intrapersonal comfort and intellectual level'. *Developmental Psychology*, 2, 335–50.
Rubin, K. (1973) 'Egocentrism in childhood: a unitary construct?' *Child Development*, 44, 102–10.
Rubin, K., Hultsch, D. and Peters, D. (1971) 'Non-social speech in four year old children as a function of birth order and interpersonal situation'. *Merrill-Palmer Quarterly*, 17, 41–50.
Salatas, H. and Flavell, J. (1976) 'Perspective taking: the development of two components of knowledge'. *Child Development*, 47, 103–9.
Sarbin, T. (1954) 'Role theory'. In Lindzey, G. (ed.) *Handbook of Social Psychology*, Vol. 1, Cambridge, Mass.: Addison-Wesley.
Scaife, M. and Bruner, J. (1975) 'The capacity for joint visual attention in the infant'. *Nature*, 253, 265–6.
Selman, R. (1970) 'The importance of reciprocal role-taking for the development of conventional moral thought'. Unpublished paper, Graduate School of Education, Harvard University.
- (1973) 'A structural analysis of the ability to take another's social perspective: stages in the development of role-taking ability'. Paper presented at the meeting of the Society for Research in Child Development, Philadelphia.
Shantz, C. (1975) 'The development of social cognition'. In Hetherington, E. (ed.) *Review of Child Development Research*, Vol. 5, Chicago: University of Chicago Press.

Shantz, C. and Watson, J. (1971) 'Spatial abilities and spatial egocentrism in the young child'. *Child Development*, **42**, 171–81.

Shatz, M. and Gelman, R. (1973) 'The development of communication skills: modifications in the speech of young children as a function of listener'. *Monographs of the Society for Research in Child Development*, **38**, No. 5.

Staub, E. (1971) 'The use of role-playing and induction in children's learning of helping and sharing behaviour'. *Child Development*, **42**, 805–16.

Shotter, J. (1974) 'The development of personal powers'. In Richards, M. (ed.) *The Integration of a Child into a Social World*. Cambridge: The University Press.

Steward, M. and Steward, D. (1973) 'The observation of Anglo-, Mexican- and Chinese-American mothers teaching their young sons'. *Child Development*, **44**, 329–37.

Stott, D. (1971) *Bristol Social Adjustment Guides Manual*, 4th edition. London: The University Press.

Stryker, S. (1967) 'Symbolic interaction as an approach to family research'. In Manis, J. and Meltzer, B. (eds.) *Symbolic Interaction*. Boston: Allyn and Bacon.

Swift, J. (1964) 'Effects of early group experience'. In Hoffman, M. and Hoffman, L. (eds.) *Review of Child Development Research*. New York: Russell Sage.

Terman, L. and Merrill, M. (1961) *The Stanford Binet Intelligence Scale: Manual for the third revision, form L-M*. London: George Harrap.

Urberg, K. and Docherty, E. (1976) 'Development of role-taking skills in young children'. *Developmental Psychology*, **12**, 198–203.

Van de Geer, J. (1971) *Introduction to multivariate analysis for the social sciences*. San Francisco: Freeman.

Van Lieshout, C., Leckie, G. and Smits-Van Sonsbeek, B. (1973) 'The effect of a social perspective taking training on empathy and role-taking ability of preschool children'. Paper presented at the meeting of the International Society for the Study of Behavioural Development, Ann Arbor, Michigan.

Voyat, G. (1973) 'The work of Henri Wallon'. *International Journal of Mental Health*, **1**, 4–23.

Vygotsky, L. S. (1962) *Thought and Language*. Cambridge, Mass.: MIT Press.

Wallon, H. (1947) *Les Origines de la Pensée chez L'Enfant*. Paris: Presses Universitaires de France.

Watzlawick, P., Beavin, J. and Jackson, D. (1968) *Pragmatics of Human Communication*. London: Faber and Faber.

Weinheimer, S. (1972) 'Egocentrism and social influence in children'. *Child Development*, **43**, 567–78.

Wentink, E., Smits-van Sonsbeek, B., Leckie, G. and Smits, P. (1975) 'The effect of a social perspective-taking training on role-taking ability and social interaction in preschool and elementary school children'. Paper presented at the Third Biennial Meeting of the International Society for the Study of Behavioural Development: Guildford, England.

West, H. (1974) 'Early preschool interaction and role-taking skills: an investigation in Israeli children'. *Child Development*, **45**, 1118–21.

Zahn-Waxler, C., Radke-Yarrow, M. and Brady-Smith, J. (1977) 'Perspective taking and prosocial behaviour'. *Developmental Psychology*, **13**, 87–8.